TITO'S LITTLE PIONEER

GROWING UP IN YUGOSLAVIA

COLLECTION OF TRUE STORIES
FIRST THROUGH FOURTH GRADES

ESTER ELLIOTT

ISBN-13:978-1533004291
ISBN-10:1533004293
CreateSpace Independent Publishing
Printed in USA

To
Apu and Anyu

CONTENTS

Socialist Federal Republic of Yugoslavia

Subotica

1965 – 1969

PROLOGUE

At the beginning of WWII, Germany attacked and occupied the Kingdom of Yugoslavia. The king fled abroad, taking the country's treasures with him. The Yugoslav army was unprepared to protect the people. Josip Broz Tito, with the help of the Soviet Communist Party unified the freedom fighters of the resistance into a partisan liberation army. Under his leadership, they fought many heroic battles. At great sacrifice they freed the country.

By the end of the war millions of Yugoslavs had died and everything was in ruins. People didn't want the king to return and rule because he betrayed them and never sent any help during the fighting. They choose Josip Broz Tito to be their leader. Tito promised a new society without class differences, a new way of life where everyone would be equal. He urged all nations and nationalities to work together in rebuilding this new country, which he called the Socialist Federal Republic of Yugoslavia.

Twenty years have passed since then.

My story begins during first grade in Subotica, a town near the Hungarian border. In this town the majority of the people were Hungarians. I was one of them.

1

Tito's Voice on Radio: *It's our responsibility as a country, and as a Party, to raise these children as trustworthy pioneers in a spirit of brotherhood and unity.*

Comrades, in the past twenty years we built roads and railroads, dams and power plants, factories, hospitals, and schools. We have almost 18 million Yugoslav people which consist of six nations and seven nationalities, all equal, all with equal rights to education in their native language. We will have a five year plan for physical education, cultural development, and science. The new referendum of the Pioneer Union of Yugoslavia emphasizes the importance of education reforms. Now we will build more schools because, dear comrades, the children are our country's future.

PIONEER PLEDGE

We were to become pioneers. On the day of the ceremony we stood in the amphitheater on a low podium. I smoothed out my blue skirt and buttoned up the top button on my white blouse. I didn't want the collar to tangle up when I got my red scarf.

Like all the kids in the country, I began first grade at age seven. Before November 29th, the Republic Day holiday, schools held initiation ceremonies all over

Yugoslavia.

There were twenty-six Hungarian and twenty-six Serbo-Croatian pupils in first grade. The amphitheater was filled with students from grades 2 through 8. All of them wore their red scarves except us.

The teachers were standing by the side walls, watching us. We were told earlier not to yawn, fidget or talk during the ceremony. When a teacher looked at you with arching eyebrows, you knew you were doing something wrong. Other teachers were in the audience making sure everyone behaved.

I smelled fresh paint. My school was a new building, not quite finished. The workers were still painting and installing sinks in the lavatories, but we attended classes.

During the swearing-in ceremony we would be required to answer questions and I was a little nervous because everybody was watching. I wished my mother was here but she wasn't invited. This was an official school event. My palms began to sweat when teacher Bezzegh left the amphitheater.

The previous day she told us we should answer with a loud 'yes' to show enthusiasm. The head of the Pioneer Union would come to the school and he could ask anything, but the answer was always to be 'yes.' We were worried that if the man changed the questions and the answer should be 'no' we wouldn't become pioneers.

Teacher Bezzegh waved her hand at this idea and said, "That never happens. This is more of a formality, not a test. Everyone becomes a pioneer when they start first grade."

How horrible it would be if I gave the wrong answer

because I didn't understand the Serbo-Croatian question.

Teacher Bezzegh said, "They'll ask you in Hungarian."

We thought we might not understand that either, if it was like the speeches on the radio. She explained with a gesture, "I'll nod my head so you will know what to say."

We had rehearsed during class how to say 'yes' together. We started out quietly. Teacher Bezzegh was lifting her arms up and up until we shouted. She lowered her arms. "Enough. I don't want you to get hoarse for tomorrow."

We were still waiting in the amphitheater. All the kids in the audience had red scarves. I couldn't imagine what would happen if I didn't become a pioneer. What if I ended up as the only one without a scarf?

I was relieved when teacher Bezzegh returned.

She whispered to her colleagues. "The clutch is stuck on his Fiat. He'll be late because he's riding his bike from Aleja Marshala Tita."

She turned to us. "Let's sing *Pioniri Maleni*." She began and we joined in.

Pioniri maleni,
mi smo vojska prava.
Svakog dana rastemo,
k'o zelena trava.

Smrt fašizmu,
a sloboda narodu.
I mene ce moja mati
pionirom zvati.

Little Pioneers,
we are a real army.
Every day we grow,
like green grass.

Death to fascism,
and freedom to the people.
My mother will call me
a pioneer.

I unbuttoned the top button of my blouse. It was choking me. I knew we would sing for a while because this man, the head of the Pioneer Union, lived on the opposite end of town in the new high-rise built by the government.

After half an hour a stranger came in, his forehead sweaty. He was dressed like a soldier. I hadn't seen this kind of uniform during any military parades. It reminded me of the partisan movies. The moss-colored jackets were fuzzy and warm so they could sleep in the forest while waiting for the Nazis. But this stranger was wearing a red scarf.

I was surprised when he said he was from the Pioneer Union because he was as old as my father. Only little kids could be pioneers. After fifteen you would be in a Youth Organization.

He talked about how children helped win the war, then added, "They sneaked through enemy lines and carried messages to warn Tito and his partisans. Many of them sacrificed their lives for you. Remember them, and be grateful that you live in peace."

I wasn't sure what to do to show gratefulness, but this wasn't the time to ask questions. When I thought of the kids who died so I could go to school I felt a lump in my throat. I tried to undo the button at my neck but it was already open.

He looked at us. "Your teachers explained why you're here today. Right?"

Some of us glanced at teacher Bezzegh. She smiled and moved her chin a tiny bit but I could see the answer was 'yes.' We shouted in Hungarian, *"Igen!"*

The Serbo-Croatian kids yelled, *"Da!"*

The man in uniform smiled. "Today being a pioneer means to be a diligent student, and to follow the codes of honesty, loyalty and bravery of the first pioneers. The Socialist Federative Republic of Yugoslavia is your homeland and you are the future workers who will make this country great. Participate in sporting events, cultural programs, festivals and all activities planned by the Pioneer Union. Our goal is to raise a generation in a spirit of brotherhood and unity; the future workers of our homeland who will be able to carry the relay baton of freedom and prosperity which was first carried by the pioneers at the end of World War II."

I was looking forward to the interesting programs until he mentioned WWII. I remembered the TV newsreel from 1945. A man, leaning on a broken horse cart wore a coat and one sleeve didn't have an arm in it. The soldier, head bandaged, sat on a tank, waving. The kids ran with a baton through rows of bombed out houses. Tired looking people, some on crutches, others with eye patches and bandages, cheered. Several buildings were nothing more than a pile of bricks with charred window frames. That happened long ago, and I was glad that now there were no tanks on the streets.

The man from the Pioneer Union walked in front of us like he was inspecting an army. I was afraid he would ask me a question, like if I was ready to cross enemy lines with a secret message. I moved left to hide behind the girl in front of me.

His face was serious when he asked us, "Do you want to become a member of the Pioneer Union?"

Teacher Bezzegh nodded but we were already shouting, "Igen! Da!" The kids who said "Da" raised their fists too. The leader smiled at them. I didn't know if we were supposed to do it or not. We yelled again "Igen!" to make sure the leader heard us too.

Some of the teachers stood by the wall with downcast eyes, others sighed and fidgeted. I wondered if we should have raised our fists when we said, "Yes!"

We all received a red scarf and a blue Titovka hat. I was glad that the cap covered only the top of my head and I would be able to wear a bow in my short hair.

Several teachers helped us with the scarves. I learned to tie the special knot in class but now it took me a long time to make it right. I smelled Atrix hand cream when a teacher energetically pulled on the ends of my scarf and adjusted the knot. I didn't know her. When I put on the blue partisan style Titovka hat teacher Bezzegh moved a lock of my hair and patted my face. Both the scent of talcum powder and her soft touch reassured me that my pioneer uniform was in order and I was ready for the vow.

The leader read the pioneer oath in Serbo-Croatian and some of the kids repeated after him. Then a teacher read it in Hungarian and we repeated after her,

"Today when I'm becoming a Pioneer
I give my honorable Pioneer word
that I will diligently learn and work,
respect parents and teachers
and be a faithful and honest friend
who keeps his word of honor;
that I will follow the path of the best Pioneers,
appreciate the glorious deeds of Partisans
and all progressive people of the world
who stand for liberty and peace;
that I will love my Homeland
self-managing socialist Yugoslavia
and its brotherly nations and nationalities,
and that I will build a new life,
full of happiness and joy."

The leader rubbed his eyes and said with trembling voice, "Welcome to the Pioneer Union of Yugoslavia."

All the teachers smiled and everyone applauded. As the kids in the audience stood up, the wooden seats folded up with a rapid bang-bang. The man in uniform was startled as he was surrounded by kids pushing towards the entrance. He was laughing, afraid to move, until the teachers ushered him out. I heard him say "war zone" while I hurried to the hallway to get a bottle of Cokta.

At home I didn't get to drink Cokta or any other sweet sodas. Mother called them factory made bubbling trash.

But I knew she thought it was too expensive. Father's chauffeur salary was low.

The tables in the hall were covered with crisply ironed white tablecloths. Salty biscuits, tiny sandwiches, pastries and various drinks had been prepared for us, the newly initiated pioneers. Little paper flags and flowers made the tables even prettier. Teachers were laughing and congratulating us.

I wondered what other activities the Pioneer Union would offer to us. Would they always give us good snacks and decorate the tables with roses and carnations? When I took the last bite of my chocolate mignon I realized I wasn't a little kid anymore who was just playing at home. I was in school. I had a uniform and I had become a little pioneer. I felt special because I was like every other seven-year-old.

Over Time:

The word pioneer connected us to the brave children of WWII. They couldn't play and study like we did. We wrote essays and drew pictures telling about them. The teachers told us we honored them by being diligent students.

Throughout my school years I heard many times how lucky we were to live in peace, and that was the greatest gift a country could offer its people.

Radio: *"Each year we publish more than 6000 book titles, in over 40 million copies. We attained great results and the Communist Party continues its fight to provide education for all the people," said the head of the Culture Ministry, Boris Popovich.*

MOTHER HOLLE

In 1st grade on the first day of school teacher Bezzegh said, "The most important thing is that this year you learn to read Hungarian. Reading is the basis of all knowledge."

Then we drew circles, triangles, semi-circles but all the shapes had to remain between two lines.

The second day of school the teacher said, "You'll learn to write the letters of the alphabet." She looked at us with a smile when she opened the book called 'My First Reader.'

"You'll read short words, short sentences, then continue with longer words and longer sentences. By New Year you'll read whole stories."

I knew a great mystery was going to be revealed to me. Learning to read was the most serious step of my entire seven years of life.

The teacher hung a huge scroll over the blackboard and carefully unrolled it. The yellowed paper had letters and pictures. Each letter had its own square.

I gazed at the ragged scroll thinking, *Wow, this is the key to knowledge.*

Teacher Bezzegh pointed at the picture of the apple and we said *'alma.'* With white chalk she wrote the capital 'A' and lowercase 'a' on the blackboard. She also showed us how to hold the pencil properly. In our lined notebooks we had to write a whole row of 'Aa.' She walked around checking how we did and I smelled the fresh soap on her freckled hand when she stopped to look at my work.

Then she pointed at the picture of a bean and we said *'bab.'* She taught us how to write letter 'B.'

I tried very hard to draw the letters properly and keep them between the lines. By the end of the class my fingers were stiff. I had trouble with the small 'a.'

Teacher Bezzegh smiled at us. "For homework, finish the whole page of 'a' and 'b.' When you write the letter, say it out loud. Listen to the sound." She had wavy honey-brown hair and her dark skirt was wider than my mother's. Her eyes smiled even when she was serious.

Gently, she folded up the yellow scroll. I knew that it was the most important map, one which would help me discover the whole world. But my letters looked different in the notebook. I was eager to practice.

The third day of school the teacher pointed at the horse and we said *'lo.'* When we asked why we skipped to letter 'l' she reassured us, "You'll learn all 40 letters plus 4 more which are only used to write foreign words." She pointed at Xylophone, Yo-yo, WC and a scale with 100kg weights for letter 'Q.'

I ignored the four extra letters. I had trouble drawing a

nice round 'b.'

That day we read using the letters we learned. *'baba, bab, lo, ollo'* and many more. I tried to say 'be' since that was the name of the letter. I often got confused because in reading, it was just 'b.'

We continued with new letters and by the end of the first week of school I could read lots of words. We also played with the letters and grouped them into made-up words such as 'bla-bla', 'bobo', 'tla', 'tao' and others. When we read them we couldn't stop laughing.

The following Monday I went to the hospital to have my tonsils taken out. This surgery was scheduled in spring because I often had tonsil infections. The doctor said, "They aren't necessary. It's better to get rid of them so she won't need all those penicillin injections. It's easier to cure a sore throat. Most kids have this operation, no need to worry." Mother signed up my three-year-old sister Gizi too, so she wouldn't get tonsillitis anymore.

At the hospital they took my sister into the operating room first. I was in pajamas sitting on a cold bench. On the wall was a poster of a *baby-tea* with caraway-seeds and I looked for familiar letters. The corridor smelled like rotten onions and the noise of the scratching metal scared me. I was practicing letter 'b', with my finger drawing it on my palm, when the door opened. A nurse carried the limp body of Gizi away. I had never seen her this lifeless.

Soon I was lying on a cold white bed, and a man in a mask asked me, "Can you count?" Loudly I began "1, 2" and as I took a deep breath, a smelly gauze covered my face. I said "3" and everything turned black, then I woke up with a terrible sore throat. I was in a large room with rows and rows of cribs and kid-sized beds. I was very cold and wished my mother was there. Each time I swallowed it felt like a knife in my throat. I threw up chunky black stuff.

The nurse said, "You swallowed a lot of ether. It's to inhale only but you probably opened your mouth."

I thought about the ABC scroll and wondered which letter we learned that day. I cried until I fell asleep.

I stayed out of school for more than a week. It was hard to catch up with homework. It was difficult learning to draw all the new letters. For a week the teacher wouldn't ask me to read because I was still in pain and could only whisper.

We started to learn the double letters, like 'ny' for 'nyul', ty for 'tyuk.' As we chanted the letters, I gazed at the pictures of the rabbit and the chicken.

After my throat healed I read in class. The teacher said "Esztike, you stammer when you read. You need to learn the letters."

When I told mother she sighed. "Because you missed school. The doctors were on vacation so I couldn't get you in during summer."

Six weeks later we began to read whole sentences. I was still getting comments in my ABC notebook such as "Don't stutter!" and "Can't read." When I saw a letter I had to think which one it was so I could say it. I paused at each syllable and by the time I remembered the letter I couldn't understand what I read.

Teacher Bezzegh said, "Esztike, practice reading at home." Her eyes smiled as she added. "Keep doing it. That's the only way to learn it."

So I looked around the house for what else I could read. I found a newspaper called 'Magyar Szo' and two cookbooks. We didn't have any other books.

The first one was the 'Fakanal' with a wooden spoon on the cover.

I sat at the kitchen table and read slowly 'Csirke Paprikas.' After 'hagyma' there was a word of more than ten letters. I tried to guess how to use the onions but I couldn't put all the letters into one word.

I couldn't concentrate so I turned off the radio. Mother listened to the news, radio plays and music all day long because it helped her doing housework.

I leafed through the yellowish pages and found interesting drawings of kitchen tools. I didn't know what they were.

Mother walked in with a bowl of freshly shelled peas. I asked her, "Do we have an 'alma ha-mo-zo'?" and pointed at the apple-peeler.

"No" she replied.

"Did you read this whole book?" I asked.

"I know how to cook. I only use the recipes to look up measurements for cakes and biscuits."

Next was a long list of words like sauté and steam. I knew you could bake, boil and fry food but I didn't remember if I tried food made these other ways.

"Have you sautéed potatoes?" I asked.

"That's fancy French cooking. I don't have time for it."

"What about steaming the peas?"

"I'm making a soup. Do your homework!"

Mother liked to boil everything and I wondered how French cooking tastes.

I found the word 'kream' and I remembered the cherry creams with wafers. The next word was a difficult one, 'ssspee-not.' Spinach!?

I closed the book.

I opened the second one called 'Finom Etelek,' a collection of fine meals. It had a hard pink cover.

After I found my favorite page I read the word 'grill' and could almost smell the sizzling lamb patty.

I tried the next one "effefa-sirt." I always forgot that the letter is called 'ef' but you read it 'f.'

Mother sighed.

"When are we going to grill?" I asked.

"The grill is for restaurants," I continued to read with a stutter.

She was peeling carrots on a newspaper and the shreds were flying everywhere, hitting the plastic lace curtain on the window. She mumbled, "For Dr. Feher it was a routine operation. Why did I listen to him? Doctors, teachers, all the learned people ..."

The juicy carrot bits tickled my nose. I sneezed.

"I need the table to cook." Then she added softly, "Go, try the newspaper."

She turned on the radio and the reporter said, "We visited the new cafeteria in the Pioneer Chocolate factory and asked the workers' opinion about the quality of the meals."

I went in the living room and started to read the front page of the 'Magyar Szo.' We only bought the Sunday issue of the 'Hungarian Word' because that's when father had time to read it.

After a few sentences I had no idea what I read but I turned the page and continued on. I didn't know that learning could be this hard. I was yawning when Eva came home. She stroked my hair and smiled at me. She was a student at the Teacher Training College and rented a room in our house.

I looked at the photo of a man driving a tractor on a field. After I read the word 'ttttrak-tor' I couldn't find any other short words.

Next day in school I got another 'Reading is unsatisfactory' comment. It was late October and I still didn't make progress. As I walked home, through my tears I could see the yellowing hawthorn trees. I usually jumped up to catch the falling leaves but now I was thinking that I didn't like to go to school anymore, and remembered the time when I was so excited to start it.

When I arrived home and closed the gate, the window opened and Eva leaned out. She smiled, "Esztike, I have a gift for you. These were my favorite stories, I hope you'll like them." I had to stand on my toes to reach her hand.

"It's called 'Grimm's Nicest Fairy Tales.' Have you read them?" she asked. It was a new book. I could smell the fresh paper.

I shook my head 'no.' "Thank you very much."

When I looked through it, I sighed. The pages had color drawings and many words. I would be in 3rd grade by the time I finish all 225 pages.

I liked one of the pictures very much. It was a tower-like house reaching to the sky and a girl was shaking out a pillow. Her long blonde braids had tiny red bows. Below her window was a village where snow was falling. I wondered why snow fell from a pillow. The title of the story was 'Mother Holle.'

"Could you read me this one?" I asked mother.

She was cleaning the bathroom and said, "Yes, in the evening."

My little sister, Gizi burst through the door, her hands sticky with sand and mud. I hurried to the glass cabinet and put my new book next to the porcelain ballerina.

I played on the swing outside, watched the leaves falling, then stood in front of the cabinet staring at my book. I leafed through it checking out the drawings, thinking *That's a very big pillow. How could she sleep on it?*

Then I began to read Mother Holle. I read each sentence slowly and many times. I got very tired by the end of the first page. I wanted to ask mother to read it to me but she was sweeping the yard.

I wanted to know if the girl could make it snow the next day. So I turned the page. I concentrated on every word, repeated them until I understood each word, each sentence. At the end I was happy that she did a good job and got all the gold.

Before I closed the book I saw another drawing. The princess was running away from a frog with a crown. Next day mother was busy ironing, so again I couldn't ask for help. I sighed and began to read about the frog, slowly. If the sentence was long or there was a difficult word by the time I saw the period I forgot what was at the beginning of the sentence. I started over many times.

I liked going to school again. The comments I received were 'getting better' and 'can read.' Teacher Bezzegh smiled at me. "Esztike, you're very diligent."

By the time I finished 'Grimm's Nicest Fairy Tales' I didn't have any reading problems. Snow began to fall and mother was planning New Year's Eve dinner.

Over Time:

During my school years I learned several new languages. Once I knew the alphabet I was able to read Serbo-Croatian too even if I didn't understand the words.

When we learned the Cyrillic alphabet I struggled reading Serbian text. Then Flash Gordon and other comic strips in the Cyrillic *Zabavnik* magazine made reading fun. I was buying the 'Entertainer' long after I was reading fluently in Cyrillic.

I thought reading in English would be easier since I knew my ABCs. In fifth grade I found out that to read in English I had to learn the spelling of each word beforehand.

Our Latin teacher in high school demanded that we read Latin just like we would learn any living language. Later when I began French lessons, I struggled with reading. When I applied what I learned in Latin, all of a sudden pronunciation and grammar rules made sense.

During high school I joined the Esperanto Club, hoping to master a simplified new language which would be used around the world. It was revolutionary and I was ready to join the movement. I was told we had eighty members. I got a ten page booklet, with samples of grammar showing how easy it would be to read. There was no dictionary because the International Esperanto Organization was still defining the words. Months later we still didn't have any books and the six of us sat around talking about how we could help to spread a universal language. For each meeting six members showed up but they were always different people. I thought this revolution would be a failure. Existing high-class languages would win and the struggle to read would go on.

Radio: *The Bureau of People's Standard of Living issued a new referendum on how to increase sports activities in schools and factories. They also addressed all aspects of health, such as the mandatory medical checkup, nutrition, leisure-time activities and safety.*

The Pioneer Union and the Forum publishing company held a reading and poetry competition in the province of Vojvodina. Elementary school Jovan Jovanovic Zmaj in Subotica received fifty books for the school library and a trophy for the second prize.

MAGIC OF READING

I was in front of our house building a snowman, thinking about Grimm's fairy tales. Father opened the iron gate, pushing his bicycle.

"I'm going to get smoked ham. They sell the best at the Boros-ranch," he said. He had a crate tied to his seat. I knew he was saving up for the holiday meat but how big was the ham going to be? "I'll buy carrots too," he said. We ate a lot of boiled carrots.

I threw a snowball at him. He laughed as he scooped up a fistful of snow and showered me with snowflakes.

I watched the bicycle tracks and father's footsteps in the snow, which disappeared at the corner.

Our neighbor, Auntie Confectionery leaned out from her window and called me. "Esztike, I have something for you."

Her house had a shiny stone foundation and the window frames were dark green. She held out a book. She looked like one of the drawings in Mother Holle.

"This was my boys' favorite book, but they don't need it anymore. You can have it," she said.

The boys were old. In summer they came home after dark, holding hands with girls and kissing them under the hawthorn trees.

Pages were slipping out from the ragged cover. "Three boys read it but it has all the pages." She smiled.

I stood on my toes to reach the book. She had flour on her wrist and her fingers smelled of vanilla.

It was the *1001 Arabian Nights Nicest Tales*. "Thank you very much. Happy New Year!" I said and hurried home to protect my second book from snow.

It had 20 stories on 250 pages. I wondered how thick the book would be with 981 more tales.

When I read the *Little Kadi* story I felt like I was the Grand Vizier, walking with the caliph, Harun el Rasid in the bazaars of Baghdad. It felt almost as real as going with my mother to the vegetable market except buying parsnips and beets wasn't as exotic as tasting olives in Bagdad.

By the time I finished the last story I had fallen in love with reading.

Over Time:

I always had a passion for travel. Reading books made me feel like taking a trip to a place and time I couldn't visit otherwise.

For a long time I searched for the remaining 981 tales but I was told they were only available in Arabic. After the fall of the Iron Curtain, Hungary's publishing business blossomed and one of their major works was the newly translated Arabian Nights in seven volumes. I read them all.

Tito's Voice on Radio: *Since the war, the populations' social-economic structure changed drastically. Before the war 85% of the people worked in agriculture. We successfully reduced that number to one third by building our industry. People moved to the cities to work in the new factories.*

We built and rebuilt over 200,000 km of roads and railroads. Increased the capacity of the Davograd hydroelectric plant on river Drava. We began to build the Iron Gate on the Danube with our Romanian neighbors. It's going to be the largest hydroelectric plant in the world. Comrades, we should be proud of our achievements and proud of our abilities of what we could accomplish together.

Child: Anyu, how tall is the Iron Gate?
Mother: Don't worry about that, eat your breakfast.
Child: Is it taller than the city hall's tower?
Mother: When the time comes, you'll learn everything.

MAYDAY CELEBRATIONS (1966)

I tightened the tulle bows on my pigtails, then adjusted my new blue skirt.

The schoolyard was a sea of blue hats, red scarves and white shirts. Giggles, laughter, Hungarian and Serbo-

Croatian words filled the air. Most of the girls wore bows in their hair.

I was among my friends. Marti turned to me and said with a melodious voice. "I'd like to go to a picnic one day. Did you ever cook in the forest or on the meadow?"

"At the edge of the forest," I replied. "We sat on a blanket to eat in the meadow, that's why it's called a picnic."

Magdi giggled. "Probably wasn't enough room for all the blankets. The whole factory came?"

I shrugged, "Different factories. Lots of people in the forest, too."

Otti parted her long bangs then said, "I have to be at the train station by two o'clock. We'll travel four hours because grandma's village is on the other side of the *Tisza*."

"You're not going to have a picnic either?" Magdi sighed, scratching her freckled nose. "At granny's house we'll sit and eat at the table, like any other day. Except the table is under the willow. Are you bringing your jump rope?" she asked Marti. They were cousins who celebrated everything together. Marti nodded.

Vali frowned. "We have to go to the company picnic because father is a boss of four people. Then we can have our own cookout at grandma's." For any special occasion Vali wore a new outfit but she never made a big deal about that. I noticed the cuff on her blouse was double folded. Her mother was a seamstress who always made stylish clothes.

As the first graders lined up teacher Bezzegh said, "We'll join the upper grade students in front of Partizan,

24

the gymnastics club, then walk all the way to the Square of the Victims of Fascism."

She handed us small paper flags, glued to wooden sticks. I was looking forward to being in the May Day parade for the first time. Two by two in a row we headed towards the town center.

Otti pointed at a two story townhouse. "This is where I live, on the first floor."

The gray concrete building looked nicer once I knew my classmate lived there.

Teacher Bezzegh talked to Sanyi and put his torn flag in her purse. When she turned away Sanyi, with a mischievous grin, reached for Robi's flag but couldn't grab it.

We turned right onto E5. Lots of trucks drove on this international road because the Hungarian border crossing was 30 km from the town center.

I pointed to a fenced-off building across the E5. "That was my kindergarten."

A group of kindergartners behind the fence watched us. Teacher Bezzegh smiled at them. "In few months they'll start first grade. Children, wave to them. Look how sweet they are." We waved with our flags but the kids looked scared.

The kindergarten teacher showed them what to do but the kids kept staring at us. There was no traffic for a while so teacher Bezzegh smiled and talked to them across the road until the kids waved to us.

When I saw a woman in a white smock holding a baby, I whispered to Vali. "If the mother works, she leaves the baby in the back of the kindergarten. The babies cry a lot.

We had to be quiet when they slept."

Vali whispered too. "Are they sick? Do they get injections?"

I shrugged. "Their room is all white, like a hospital. And the nurses wear those cloth lace-up boots with openings for the heels and toes."

Vali declared, "The babies don't have grandmas."

Several trucks drove by. They slowed down and waved to us.

Both sides of the E5 had houses, large buildings and sidewalks. Our side had a bike path next to the sidewalk. Across the road there were tram tracks which went to Lake Palic, 7 km from the town.

We passed by an orphanage called *Kolevka*. I liked the name, which meant *Cradle* but the place itself scared me. The modern square building was on a mound, tucked away from the road. Tall grass and weeds grew in front of it, then there was a steep drop to the road. If I had to pass by I always hurried.

Magdi looked inquisitively at Marti. "I overheard mother saying that auntie will bring a surprise. What is it?"

Marti shrugged.

Magdi stared at her. "You know. Tell me."

Marti tilted her head. "A cake?"

Magdi waved, bubbling with laughter, "I know! It's a walnut cake, with plum jam and chocolate cream."

"That was the surprise." Marti smiled.

Magdi frowned. "Sounded like it was more."

In front of the orphanage a kid stood among the weeds staring down the slope at me. As I hurried up, I stepped on Marti's heel. More kids emerged from the tall grass. A bitter taste spread in my mouth and I didn't understand what Marti had just said.

Teacher Bezzegh stopped and waved to the kids. She said to us, "Children, smile and wave to them." We waved with our flags but they didn't smile, just stared at us.

Our teacher clapped her hands and shouted, "Hip-hip, hurrah!" with arms raised up. We imitated her until the toddlers smiled and clapped their hands. We were ready to leave but teacher Bezzegh was still looking at the kids hiding in the grass. "They just want to laugh like all of you. Don't be afraid of them. Smile."

"Are they going to grow up here?" asked Magdi. Teacher Bezzegh replied, "A family will adopt them. People who can't have babies or who want more children. They're adorable. They won't stay here long."

I was surprised when she said that because I saw that some were bigger than I was. If nobody wanted the kids they grew up here. When I was going home from kindergarten sometimes a nurse in a white coat was smoking a cigarette in the distance and the kids stood in the tall grass near the road. They all looked very sad and when I noticed them I wanted to cry. I thought if my parents died I would end up in that scary building.

Teacher Bezzegh waved and pointed to the windows at the far end. "See the babies and the nurses?"

I was pushing Marti in front of me to move but she couldn't because teacher Bezzegh turned back again waving to the toddlers. They had runny noses and oversized pants with diapers bulging out, the size of a soccer ball. They waddled and fell over as they headed towards us. The nurses picked them up before they could plummet over the edge. Some grabbed onto the weeds, trying to follow us. The kids scared me and I waved my flag harder to get a smile so we could leave.

Magdi whispered to me, "They should put ribbons in their hair and wipe their noses or else they'll live here forever. How hard is it?"

I wanted to believe that they would soon be adopted but I had seen them a year ago and they were still here.

Magdi shook her head. "What's wrong with the nurses? Did you see the snot was crusty all over the kid's face? Granny said she would take care of me if something should happen to my parents. I don't have to worry about this."

My grandmother was sick. I hoped my parents didn't die so I wouldn't end up in one of the cradles.

Teacher Bezzegh took my hand and her soft touch helped me believe that she was right and the lonely kids would move in with nice families. We finally continued to walk.

Next to the modern Kolevka building was the old church, called Jesus the Worker. The gates to the churchyard were closed. I wondered where the priest was.

The teacher patted my face and let go of my hand but I still felt her warm touch.

Magdi was watching Sanyi and Robi fighting over a flag. Then the teacher put the flag in her purse.

Marti whispered to me in her melodic tone, "The surprise is a tablecloth for auntie. It's orange with blue flowers, her favorite colors. Don't tell."

This was a secret and now I was excited about the

surprise. Marti continued, "Father also bought three oranges. I ate one, mother and father shared one. And the third is for the decoration on the cake. The orange peel is chopped and is soaking in rum."

When she talked I could taste the cake. A bite into a spongy walnut cake layered with buttery cream is full of surprise from the speckles of flavorful orange peel.

Teacher Bezzegh pointed across the E5. "Look, all the workers are coming to celebrate with us. Wave your flags."

The gates of the Suboticanka juice factory opened and people hurried out. Many got on bicycles. These people made Cockta and Juppi, my favorite sodas, so I waved my flag and smiled at them. Some looked at us, others talked and didn't notice us.

I liked the name of the factory, it meant a woman from Subotica. This Serbo-Croatian word had a nice melody to it.

The tram full of people rattled towards the center. We waved to them and the tram driver blew a whistle.

More trucks drove by and we cheered when they honked. On the other side of the road a group of pioneers emerged from a side street, marching and singing.

"Drugarska se pesma ori
Pesma koja slavi rad
Srce gromko nek nam zbori
Da nam zivi, zivi rad. "

Teacher Bezzegh explained, "The children who live on that side of E5 attend the October 10th school." We began to hurry so they didn't pass us. She slowed down. "No rush, the organizers lined up everyone. We'll have a place."

A truck honked. Did it honk for us? It was strange to have another group of pioneers across the road.

They didn't look at us, just sang.

"Can we sing, too?" Marti asked teacher Bezzegh.

"Later," she replied. "Enjoy the trees and the birds, now that spring is here."

We talked about the May Day picnic but kept glancing across the road.

When we walked by the Electro-remont, Vali exclaimed, "There is my dad!" He waved to us. Under his arm he had a bundle wrapped in brown paper. Vali said, "He is taking the sausages home. His colleague always brings fresh meat from the farm."

Marti pointed to the Electro-remont sign. "What do they do there?"

Vali shrugged. "Repairs. Machines. Ahh, dad always grumbles that it's impossible to get anything done. They have to wait for one screw from Slovenia."

The men leaving the factory passed us as they went to the bakery. Their fingers were greasy and their hands were full of scratches.

I said, "My father's fingernails were black when he repaired the clutch. Mother gave him a brush to scrape off the oil so he wouldn't ruin his nice hands."

Marti said, "My father works in an office. But at home he built a shed and his fingernails had dirt, too."

After we passed under the railway bridge I was certain we would get to the assembly point before the other school.

Magdi whispered, "We'll beat them. It'll take them forever to cross the E5."

Then all the trucks and buses stopped and let the other pioneers cross to our side. But at least they were behind us. Teacher Bezzegh said, "Children, lets practice the song one more time."
We sang at top of our lungs. As we passed by the police station, all the uniformed men waved to us and smiled.

"A song of comrades can be heard
A song to celebrate work
Our hearts cry out loud
Celebrate, celebrate work.
We raise our foreheads high,
We're the heroes of our work,
Railroads, villages and towns
Are the results of our hands,
The entire country will be ours,
Celebrate work, celebrate work."

As we finished the song we passed by the open windows of the Partizan wrestling team where sportsmen were training. We grimaced as we got a whiff of the sweat rising from the basement while Sanyi clung to the window pretending to faint. Teacher Bezzegh quickly led us through the sea of kids to join the upper-grade students from our school. She returned the paper flags to Sanyi and Robi.

We giggled as we watched the pioneers of the October

10th School standing near the windows of the wrestling team. At the sound of a whistle we stood up straight, flags in hand, ready for the parade.

A boy from a Youth Brigade carried the flaming red flag. Inside the big yellow star there was a hammer and sickle. The sickle looked exactly like ours. Father explained to me how to swing it to cut the grass but not stab his leg. We had many hammers at home but they were all rounded at the edges not square like the drawing on the flag.

Factory workers stood on both sides of the promenade, smiling and clapping as we passed   by. I faced them so they could see my new bows.

We often stopped because the folklore groups in the parade danced. I heard the *'Kolo naokolo'* music, which was the Serbian circle dance.

The Yugoslav flags, the ones with blue, white and red stripes with a five-pointed red star in the middle, hung on the buildings.

We passed the Pelivan ice cream shop then stopped again. Standing on the sidewalk, two young men nibbled on sunflower seeds with shells. I could never peel them with my teeth and spit it out like they did. I usually chewed the shells with the seeds and swallowed everything.

Next to them two young women clapped. Then the brunette patted the arm of the man in a striped shirt. "Laci, are you bringing the demijohn? Filled with red wine this time?"

"Sure, we're celebrating, aren't we?" He replied and forgot to spit out the sunflower shells.

She poked his arm. "Remember the bacon too, if you want to taste my cooking. I make delicious gypsy roast."

The woman in a pink dress tugged her arm. "Eva, let's go. The new shoes are here."

The woman named Eva laughed. "I clapped enough today. Hey, boys. Spread out so they don't notice a gap here." She tapped her foot on the asphalt, the sheer nylon stockings shined on her long legs.

The men spread their elbows acting like wrestlers and the one in the striped shirt winked. "Are you going to spend all your salary for shoes, comrade Eva?"

"Worker's day. Why not?" Eva smiled at him, then the two women hurried toward the store.

Her friend said, "He's already telling you how to spend your money." Eva laughed.

The men watched them disappear behind a glass door. The young man slapped Laci's arm. "You're head over ears in love. Is she the one?" They talked quietly then left, leaving a gap.

Otti pointed to the store behind us and a man in blue overalls pushing a dolly loaded with boxes. "That's the Solid shoe store. Mama said they'll bring the new models out today. They have golden ribbons on the tops."

Her parents worked at the Solid shoe factory, which was only a few streets away.

Otti continued, "All the stores will stay open the whole afternoon. It is payday in the factories."

We walked and sang when Vali shook her flag towards her mother and brother standing on a sidewalk.

Then I noticed my parents and my sister, Gizi. I waved and they cheered. I was happy they saw me in the parade.

Mother said to me, "Afterwards you can come home by yourself."

Other times I went to the center only with my parents. I pondered if I could find my way home, then I realized, yes, I could do it alone.

Teacher Bezzegh said to our parents, "Have a nice May Day!"

We walked and sang then stopped near the Victims of Fascism Square. People filled the intersection, and our class got wedged between the adults. I saw lots of hands, calluses, and soft white skin, red nail polish and gold wedding bands.

We gathered around teacher Bezzegh who lead us through the crowd to stand by the wall. She said, "We won't be able to get closer. They have speeches and dances at the monument."

The biggest church in town, St. Teresa Cathedral, was next to the square. People stood on its stairs and I asked a man, "What's happening at the monument?" He bent down, grabbed my waist and lifted me up.

I was above the crowd and could see the marble monument. On the top of it was a bronze statue of a woman holding a wreath over a dead man. Bouquets of fresh flowers were lined up on the memorial. On the stairs the folk dancers stood wearing colorful costumes. A man talked into a microphone but I could hear only a few words when he shouted. There were many large flags but they didn't float in the air, just hung down on the poles. I looked up at the towers of St. Teresa Cathedral and I wondered if they would toll the bells to celebrate the workers.

I asked the man to lower me down. He said, "Not much to see, eh?" He was wrong, but I didn't want to tell him.

When the crowd began to disperse our teacher asked, "Who is coming with me back to school and who is leaving on his own?" A few kids gathered around her, the rest of us said our parents let us walk home alone and we knew the way.

She said, "Be careful when you cross the streets, the trucks are tall and the drivers may not see you. Mostly, watch out for bicycles. They carry parcels and drive fast. Have a nice May Day picnic."

I was going home alone and I felt I was now a big girl. There was so much to see! The girls had wide bows and I was looking to see how they tied them. I watched the pioneers from other schools. Some tied their scarves in a double knot or had a ring over it.

I passed by the Krakovsky pastry shop. The owner was our neighbor. I called her Auntie Confectionery. As she stood outside in her white apron, looking at the crowd, I called out "*Csokolom, cukrasz neni.*" I always greeted her with 'Kisses to you, Auntie Confectionery.'

Her tired face changed when she smiled at me. "Esztike, I was looking for you but we had lots of people in the store. I was serving customers when you passed by." I knew she was sorry and I waved my flag to cheer her up.

I said, "I'd like a scoop of ice cream but I don't have any money. Mother is either on the promenade or at home cooking dinner. She will give you the money."

As we stepped inside the deserted store she sighed. "People bought everything. We made more cakes than last year. Still it wasn't enough."

There were empty trays with powdered sugar and traces of chocolate crumbs and cherry juice.

The patisserie had six marble tables, slim chairs, a counter facing the wall where you could stand and eat. The walls were bare, except for a large mirror on one side and Tito's photo in the center.

She said, "The strudels and mignons were gone before the parade."

The ice cream boxes were empty, too. When I stood on my toes I saw three of them had a little bit on the bottom.

I got two scoops, vanilla and strawberry. She scraped out a bit of chocolate ice cream for the top.

"The weather is nice. Are you going to have a picnic?" she asked.

I beamed. "Yes, in the Kelebia forest. Last year it rained and we put the blanket over our heads, and stood under the trees. Then we went home. Where are you going for a picnic?"

She sighed. "To the kitchen. The city women don't have time to bake, and the village people come for a visit and stop for sweets. Our ice cream is very popular."

I said, "Kisses to you," and she locked the doors after me.

It was hard to walk in the crowd and eat when mother wasn't holding my hand. I stopped under a hawthorn tree to enjoy my ice cream. After the last bite, I went to the fountain to wash my sticky fingers.

I looked at the blue sky, the green leaves and I was happy spring was here because I didn't have to wear a winter coat. People smiled everywhere. When I got thirsty

I looked for a well. I knew one was at the fruit market but didn't see any on the promenade so I went home.

Mother asked me how it was, coming home alone. I told her about the ice cream and she got upset. "You shouldn't go around begging," she scolded. I shrugged. I wanted ice cream and didn't have money. I asked and I got it.

An hour later mother and I went across the street to pay my debt. Mother offered the money. "Thank you very much," she said. "Here is 20 para for the two scoops." Auntie Confectionery kept her hands in the pockets of her white apron and smiled. "No, it's all right. Rozsika, you don't owe me anything."

I was leaving but mother held up the 20 para and said, "I was taught to pay back my debts. I don't want anything for free. I know what hard work it is to run that shop."

Auntie Confectionery shook her head. "Rozsika, I'm mixing the apricot filling for tomorrow's strudels, I have to go. Don't worry, it's all right." She left.

Mother held the coins and looked at me, "I'm so embarrassed. I didn't raise you to be a beggar."

I wondered what mother was talking about. I knew Auntie Confectionery liked me. She was kind, soft spoken and always smelled sweet. I was her neighbor.

We were inside the kitchen when mother said quietly. "She likes you because she has three boys and no daughter." Mother put the coins on the table. "Next time you go to town I'll give you money so you can buy one scoop of ice cream. Take this now."

I was happy she offered me money when I didn't even ask for it. I never carried my own money before unless the teacher asked us to pay for something. But now the twenty para was mine to spend. I'd ask mother to get me a purse. I couldn't remember if my summer outfits had pockets. She was still mumbling to herself. "You work day-in-day-out when you're a 'private worker.' If you are in a factory, you have free time. If you're 'private' you never have a holiday."

It was better not to ask for a new purse now, so I went to check my clothes for pockets.

Over Time:

All the way through high school I often enjoyed ice cream and pastries at the Krakovsky confectionery. Later they had a staff to serve ice cream. I always had the money, ready to pay, but if Auntie Confectionery was there and she shook her head 'no', I thanked her with a smile.

When mother asked me if I ate anything, I replied, "I tried to pay." Then she shook her head saying, "Every day they get up at three o'clock to roll out the dough and they're in the shop at six with fresh strudels. Each pastry has twelve layers of flaky dough." She couldn't stop shaking her head.

Yugoslavia ceased to exist when each Republic declared independence and became a separate country. Each one of them changed the list of national holidays. Instead of Army Day, Partisan Uprising and Republic Day they chose to celebrate Easter, All Saints Day, and Independence. If the Republic had Muslim citizens then

Ramadan became an official holiday too.

New Years Day remained from the old calendar, as well as Labor Day to celebrate International Workers Day on May 1st. Because the workers earned the right to rest, May 2nd stayed a public holiday, just like it was in the Socialist Federal Republic of Yugoslavia.

Radio: *In today's annual meeting of Communist Party of Yugoslavia president Josip Broz Tito declared: "We built housing for more than a million families but we will continue to build more. We have the cement and construction materials to use instead of importing them. In the whole country we want to develop and improve living conditions. The standard of living politics is a top priority for us and we'll fight with all our forces to resolve these burning issues."*

Dear Listeners, next is organ music played by Isaiah Alexandrovich Braudo, a Professor from the Leningrad Conservatoire.

THE CASTLE

My sister Gizi and I were in our yard, running towards the fence. I won the race again. The first time I enjoyed my win but after the fourth time I got bored. Cold wind blew and yellow leaves drifted to the ground. I headed inside.

"Again. This time I will win." Gizi spoke with such confidence that I believed her. But once we started to run I knew I'd be the first to reach the gate. I was eight years old and she was four. Our teddy bear was bigger than she was. Gizi didn't care if she lost each time, she just wanted to run.

I changed the rules. After she took off I counted to five then I ran to catch up with her. This way I wasn't sure if I could win and the contest was more interesting.

Gizi was too little to understand my life. I was in second grade, I could read and write. I agreed to play tag, hide and seek and other games we invented but I refused to wrestle with her. I was afraid I'd break her bones.

I couldn't talk to my sister the way I talked to my friends but we laughed a lot.

I said, "I'll teach you a new language. Hold your tongue with your fingers, like that. Now say something."

"Wthel iz da cer?" she asked.

"Inf da kufchen," I replied.

We headed for the house, lisping and chuckling.

The neighbor, Aunt Mancika was in the kitchen talking to mother. "Fancy that! I added ground carob to the cherries but it's too juicy for the topping. I used up all the flour in the batter and I don't have time to go to the store."

Mother filled a cup with flour.

"Thank you Rozsika, I'll return it."

She often ran out of some ingredient when she baked and I liked when she borrowed sugar or eggs or a pinch of salt. She returned it later along with a plate of her pastries. They were very good, sweeter than mother's.

Gizi and I staggered inside, whispering as we held the tip of our tongues. "Whaf do you ppfut in daa caake? Fancyy dhat, rison." I wiped the tears of laughter from my face.

Then I noticed my book, 'The Tales of the Forest' was on the wrong shelf tossed to the side.

I turned to my sister. "You can't touch my books. I told you. Mother told you."

I escorted her towards the kitchen. We stopped in front of the door when I heard mother talking to Aunt Mancika. "What am I going to do alone with two small children when the bank takes this house? Who would hire me with four years of elementary school? I couldn't pay the loan."

"My Rozsika, you'll eat yourself up. From all this worry you'll get an ulcer."

Mother sighed. "He planned to be home early morning. Now it's after five."

Aunt Mancika adjusted a lock of her chestnut color hair and said, "Probably stopped for coffee or something to eat. Slovenia is a long way."

The glass door pane was covered with lace curtains and I saw Aunt Mancika heading out. "Anyhow, this government promises help to everyone. They must have a program to help you in case -- God forbid -- something happened to Bela."

Mother waved her hand. "Government aid? We can barely meet ends with a regular salary. Bela wasn't a partisan and he isn't a party member."

"If you're one of them you could live like you were in the west." Aunt Mancika lowered her voice, "*Bitangok*." She always whispered when she called the leadership 'scoundrels' but I could still hear through the closed doors.

"When I think of snow on those narrow mountain roads." Mother rubbed her eyes.

"Try to calm down." Said Aunt Mancika as she left.

Mother always worried that something would happen to father. I didn't like it but I got used to it.

I pulled my sister in the kitchen and told mother what happened to my book.

She said, "Gizi probably looked at the pictures. Why don't you read to her?" I was disappointed that she didn't warn Gizi, or didn't explain that the big sister has a serious job; she attends school.

Mother reminded me several times that Gizi didn't have any small kids to play with. Until she started kindergarten in two years I had to play with her after my homework was done.

I knew Gizi wouldn't sit still for a whole story but I began to read 'The Prince and the Winged Horse.' I felt I had traveled to enchanted lands, that I had seen the castles and lakes.

When I read "The prince flew across Seven Seas and Seven Kingdoms," Gizi galloped around the table with arms stretched out. I couldn't imagine the winged horse so I read louder and turned my back to her. "The prince promised to kill the seven-headed dragon and bring back the golden apple."

I heard the armoire doors slamming in the bedroom, then I got a scent of quince and rosemary and heard more footsteps. I knew what Gizi did but I had to turn to see which scarf she picked out.

I rushed to the kitchen. "Gizi is playing with your scarf. The one with anchors and towers. I can't read to her."

Mother stirred the soup and called Gizi. "Put my scarf back. And listen to the story."

I wished father got home soon so mother would be cheerful again.

I curled up on the divan in the living room and sent

Gizi to the bedroom. I wanted to know what happened to the prince but I knew my sister's playing would interrupt me. I leafed through my book, unable to decide which story to read.

My eyes glazed over as I studied the room. The wavy wood pattern on the combined closet looked like the map of the Seven Kingdoms. The light shimmered on the glass cabinets and the TV sitting on a serving trolley. The large stove made of ceramic tiles looked like a fire-mountain. The flowers on the four armchairs and the tablecloth on the square table could have been the garden in the palace.

During the night this pull-out divan was my bed. My sister's crib was next to it, one side lowered because she wasn't a baby anymore.

I heard the springs creak in the bedroom where our parents slept and I knew Gizi climbed up on the 'mountain' made of goose feather comforter and large pillows. I used to play with her and slide down when mother didn't see us.

I chose the 'Goose Herder' and read it out loud. I knew this story, I could easily imagine it.

Gizi shouted. "What happened to the dragon?"

"You're too noisy. I have to read it alone," I replied.

Then I heard thumps. I had to find out what happened in the other room. I checked the little table in the corner where I did my homework. My pencil and notebook were just as I left them.

Both armoires were wide open. Gizi put on several pairs of socks then slid down the bedding, landing on the ground. "Much better in these socks." She grinned.

She grabbed more socks from the wardrobe and

messed up the clothes. "You can't wear mine." I said, moving my lace socks to a higher shelf.

My sister often said, 'I didn't know.' Little kids have to be reminded what they are allowed to do.

"Don't you play with my scarf. Clear? Wait until you get yours." Just in case, I moved my pioneer scarf to a higher shelf.

She said, "When are the *Dani Pionirske Igre*? Are you going to teach me new games?"

"Yes, but you do as I tell you. When I practice for the reading contest, you must be quiet."

In spring, during the Days of Pioneer Games, we would run an obstacle course, have activities and contests in history, art, reading, and sports. Afterwards, my sister and I would make up new games for ourselves.

The dogs barked on the street and we ran to the window, shouting, "Apu is home." But nobody was at the gate. I wished father was home so we could play. He was strong and he could spin and swing me around as long as I wanted. We all liked to wrestle with him. I stared out the window until mother called us to have supper. We raced to the kitchen.

In the hall we passed by the third room, which we weren't allowed to go in. It was rented out to students.

After supper we watched Lolka and Bolka, a Polish cartoon. The two boys didn't talk. They giggled or grunted. I loved Bolka's magic pencil. Whenever they got in trouble Bolka drew an object and it became real.

The next afternoon father walked in the kitchen, smiling. Gizi and I hugged him then took the chocolate from his pocket.

Mother's voice was low when she asked him, "Where were you?"

He waved his hand. "The director made a detour. We went to a department store to see the stockings then Uco decided to try the wild boar in this restaurant. It was in a castle."

The president of the March 8 Lace Factory had a proper name but everyone called him Uco.

Mother had an icy glare. "I couldn't sleep last night. I kept listening for the key to turn in the lock."

Father didn't smile anymore. "The manager was his old friend who tried to convince him to stay in the hotel. When Uco says, let's go, my job is to drive him. I can't tell him what to do."

"I know. You could have sent me a telegram while they were feasting."

He said, "Uco wanted to leave yesterday but his friend held us back. He offered another appetizer -- so many plates you couldn't see the tablecloth. The post office was already closed. It took forever to cook the old boar."

"Probably it was frozen." She spoke quietly. "What would become of us if something would happen to you? We would be thrown out from this house."

"I'm here." Father hugged her. "Anyway, they promised in socialism we'll always have a roof over our heads. Not like in the old days."

"Sure, this is a promised land. Bank is a bank, they want their money." Mother's voice was harsh.

He pondered. "But it's different. Now the government has a say in it. Tito knows how to keep them in a corral." He grinned. "The old man is a big dog."

She hushed him. "Not in front of the children." She stared at him. "Where did you sleep?"

"I wanted to sleep in the car but Uco wouldn't let me. He arranged it and they found a bed for me."

When father went to the basement to fix the leaky faucet, I followed him, munching on a pear. "Did you sleep in the tower?"

"Shucks!" He laughed. "It was a broom closet."

I couldn't imagine that. We had an inside broom and an outside broom but no closet.

"It had shelves and a rickety sofa, no bedding. The cleaning lady gave me a soft pillow, I wrapped my coat over me and slept like a top."

"Was it upstairs? Did you see far from the castle?" I asked.

He chuckled. "Ah, ground floor. It was a tall room with a burned out light bulb hanging off a long wire. When you closed the door it was pitch black. The shelves were full of light bulbs. The ladder was in the corner, so I thought the wiring must be damaged. In the morning when I thanked the cleaning woman for the nice pillow I asked her what was wrong with the light. She said the bulb burned out two months ago and the repairman never had time to replace it. I changed the bulb. She couldn't stop thanking me and saying how skillful I was."

He shook his head.

"Where did Uco sleep? In the tower?" I asked.

"I didn't see his room. Otocec is a fancy castle on an island in the middle of the river Krka. It's beautiful."

"Was it full of guests?"

He shrugged. "In the fall it's empty."

As I finished the pear he turned on the faucet so I could wash my sticky fingers. I was wondering how come Uco slept in a room and father got only a pillow. The sofa didn't even have sheets.

He put the wrench away and said, "The luxury hotel is for big shots and western tourists. It's not for me." I was always amazed when father could read my mind.

"That was a very good pillow. It's in every room like that. Must be nice to sleep there." He switched off the light.

Later on Gizi and I wrestled with father. We couldn't even move his legs to topple him. He stood firm like a marble statue, trying to look serious. When mother brought in the clean clothes, I yelled, "Anyu, help, we can't knock over Apu."

She tossed the clothes on the chair. "I'll get you, just wait," then grabbed his leg. Father wobbled holding back laughter.

Mother tried to twist his arm then yelled, "Grab him now." Her voice tinkled with triumph as she commanded, "Children, grab his knees. 1-2-3 now!" We were too weak from chuckling as we pulled his feet.

She called us to help but we were rolling on the floor, laughing tears. She wrestled him alone using moves we saw on TV, but father defended himself.

My jaw was numb, my face wet. I had trouble closing my mouth. I couldn't remember what was funny anymore but I couldn't stop laughing.

Mother snickered. "Eating wild boar instead of sending a telegram." She was pinching, tickling and pulling him with all her strength until he was in the corner and both of them collapsed to the floor, exhausted from laughter.

Father hugged her stroking mother's black hair. "Mamikam, I promise I will always come home. If I'm late I will send you a message."

She leaned on his shoulder and let out a deep sigh. "So how was the wild boar?"

Father waved his hand. "Dry. Uco nudged me to try it so I had a few bites from his plate. I ordered a schnitzel. What's sure is sure."

"Ahh, restaurant chefs," scoffed mother. "They *klophol* the meat real thin, dredge it in too much bread crumbs so it will look large. Sunday I'll make you a real schnitzel. We'll use the floral plates, as if we are in a castle."

I knew she would cook dinner humming along to the music on the radio because father was home. I couldn't wait to set the table.

Over Time:

Mother worried about father's travels until he retired. Then it took her some time to adjust to having him home every day.

We wrestled and rolled on the floor with laughter many more times. I thought it was normal to have a numb jaw and tears from an unstoppable laugh. Years later I realized that these moments are rare and precious, and unknown in some families.

Radio: *Teachers must instill the socialist ideas at a young age and prepare the future workers of our country for the entry into the Communist Party.*

Child: What is she saying?
Mother: Don't pay attention, this is not for children.
Child: Can I get new sandals?

PRACTICE SCHOOL AND TEACHERS-IN-TRAINING

Before I began school I thought the teachers knew everything.

I started first grade in Jovan Mikic elementary school. Next to us was a park and an unfinished four story building. In late October teacher Bezzegh lead us across the construction site and showed us the entrance. "Starting tomorrow you'll line up here, this is your school now. It's called the 'Practice School' until they decide who it should be named for. On the upper floor is the Teacher's Training College."

The gym was unfinished. The park was fenced off with sand and gravel piled up among the hawthorn trees. When we walked into the spacious classroom I was relieved the rumors were not true. The back of the chairs weren't upside down with long screws sticking out.

Most of the elementary schools were named after partisans. I hoped we would get a new name soon because 'Practice School' didn't sound like a proper place for learning. I wished I could stay in Jovan Mikic.

In second grade we had teacher Bozanich. One day she announced, "Because we're an experimental school, the Board decided that whoever your current teacher is will remain your teacher until you start fifth grade." She explained things well and I learned a lot so it was all right with me.

She was older than my mother but younger than my grandmother. She wore gray, brown, or green clothes with a colorful scarf. Her nail polish matched her lipstick. She had wrinkles between her eyebrows and was always looking for her glasses.

Extra chairs lined the back wall of our classroom, under Tito's picture. The teachers-in-training often sat there taking notes. Sometimes one of them was teaching us.

They always smiled at us and were careful not to bump into us when we rushed into the classroom. Especially if they carried chairs.

The visitors were accompanied by professor Ujhelyi. His name was interesting, it meant 'from a New Place.' He was older than my father. He always wore a suit and when he crossed his legs I could see the top of his dark socks. They had a yellow zigzag seam. I wasn't sure if father's factory made his socks or not. I could recognize the girls' stockings but didn't know much about men's socks.

He usually had a kind smile for us but he could raise

his voice if he saw Sanyi elbowing Zoli. "How would you feel if I punched you *accidently*?" he asked, and Sanyi stopped repeating it was an accident.

One day after class teacher Bozanich said to Professor Ujhelyi, "I don't use this new style you call lesson plan. They taught us differently in the old system, before the war."

He smiled, "You're an experienced teacher, you don't need to prepare notes." She blushed under her orange powder, relieved.

We were used to visitors. They were teachers who wore shorter skirts and didn't have multiple glasses. Teacher Bozanich had to change glasses when she read to us.

They called these visits 'practice', 'style', 'observation', 'sample lecture' or something else. For us everything was a regular lesson ending with homework, except the teachers-in-training couldn't give us grades so we liked it when lots of people sat in the back.

When we were alone we felt free to discuss anything with our teacher. We wanted to know what happened after the lessons, if they got a good grade. We wanted to know when our gym would be finished and asked why they had to redo the floor and walls. In 3rd grade we asked again, "When is our school going to get a proper name?"

"Soon, the Board is working on it," she replied. I couldn't understand why it would take more than two years to decide on a name.

One day, teacher Bozanich held a 'sample lesson' showing how to teach Knowledge of Nature and Society.

Lots of people were sitting under Tito's picture, taking notes.

She pointed at a drawing in the book. "The birds fly to Africa each fall because our winter is too cold for them."

Professor Ujhelyi made a comment to these visitors, his students, which had nothing to do with the birds or Africa. "This is how you awaken curiosity. You always encourage them to think."

When he talked we all turned our heads towards him. He said, "I apologize for the interruption."

Then my teacher asked questions and we answered. He would comment on that, too. "Remember, interaction is the most important method for a pedagogue. If you can't engage them you fail as an educator. Without dialog you won't understand how they think."

We were told to be quiet when he talked to his students. Most often I didn't understand what he said but I knew his favorite word was 'methodology.'

His brown socks had a yellow seam too and were a proper fit for his thin legs. I wondered if they were made in a Slovenian factory, famous for good quality. My father's socks always bulged around his ankles because the elastic got lose after the socks were washed a few times.

Teacher Bozanich asked me to read from the textbook.

I read loudly, "Each continent has a unique landscape. Migrating birds eat fruits and various seeds as they travel north or south. They spread the seeds. If a bird drops an apple seed in the Sahara desert what would people have to do to grow an apple tree? If the birds bring an orange seed from the south and drop it in your yard, what would happen to the seed?"

The professor said, "Eszter reads very well." Then he would smile at teacher Bozanich saying, "Good job." This put a twinkle in her eye and she continued.

In early spring a blonde teacher was lecturing us, the last class of the day. We were told to be cooperative because this was her only chance to practice before her big exam. It was almost six o'clock and we were waiting for the bell to ring. We were whispering about not wearing a winter coat anymore and kept looking out the window. She asked questions but when nobody raised a hand she answered the questions herself. Even Marti was packing up her books, and I barely understood what our homework was.

After class I saw teacher Bozanich coming from the back row, shaking her head. I heard her say "discipline … too quiet …" and then I was pushing my way out the door with the others. I looked back to see the young woman eagerly nodding at every word, her long curls covering her face.

A few days later the young teacher returned with her hair tied up in a bun. She was followed by her thirty classmates, many of them bringing chairs.

That week Zoli and I were on duty to keep the classroom in order and assist the teacher if she needed help. We had to make sure all the students left the classroom during the 15 minute break. That's when we opened the windows, cleaned the blackboard and got chalk from the porter, and made sure the sponge was wet. When it dried the white dust floated in the air and made us sneeze. It was hard to wipe off all the chalk; our blackboard usually looked gray. I could reach only as high as the middle of it but I'd jump up to wipe it higher.

When the young teacher came in during the break she cleaned the blackboard so well, it looked new. I didn't know it could be that dark. She washed the sponge and it was bright yellow.

No matter how many times I rinsed it, the sponge remained white and so did my fingers. To clean the white powder off you had to scrub your hands with soap, but the bathrooms rarely had proper soap. It was usually a slimy chunk which you didn't want to touch.

She even brought her own soap and soap dish then washed her hands in the sink. Professor Ujhelyi smiled at her. "Don't be nervous," he said and sat down in the back next to teacher Bozanich.

When the bell rang we were all in our seats ready for Knowledge of Nature and Society. We were reminded again not to pay attention to the people at the back wall and to participate in class like any other day.

The young teacher talked about nature in the city. I was admiring her tailored beige blouse and the burgundy lines on her checkered bell-shaped skirt.

She asked us, "Did any of you notice the birds and what they do?"

Nobody raised their hand. There was thick silence in the classroom.

I gazed at the board. It was still black after it dried. To make it black sometimes we soaked it so much that it was too slippery for the chalk and you couldn't write on it.

The teacher looked around and repeated with a trembling voice. "Did anybody notice the birds and what they do?"

Everyone was quiet as her eyes searched our faces.

I felt very uncomfortable. I raised my hand. She took a deep breath and a smile flooded her face. "Yes, tell us what you saw."

"When we took the tram to Lake Palic I noticed a stork nest on the top of the electric pole. I saw the stork flying and landing."

She said, "Storks like to nest outside of the town, close to a field and marshy area to catch food."

Suddenly many hands were up. The whole class remembered where, how and when they saw pigeons, sparrows, and crows fighting with squirrels. Everybody wanted to talk. The teacher beamed with excitement seeing so many hands in the air. "We don't have time for all of you to answer. For homework write ten sentences about the birds you noticed."

Professor Ujhelyi said loudly. "Eszter is very smart and observant." I felt a tingling inside. If he said I was smart, then it had to be true.

The young teacher talked about nature in cities, parks, and flower pots on balconies. Her voice was different and it was good to listen to her. From there on the whole class paid attention. When she ended the class with, "Next time you'll learn about plants in the city," I wished she would return for another lesson.

When the bell rang, the blonde teacher was smiling. Professor Ujhelyi shook hands with her. "Congratulations. You'll be a great teacher." She let out a deep sigh.

Her skirt was made of a fuzzy wool and it almost touched my face as I hurried to sneak out for my break.

When I lifted my head I could see her burgundy leather belt. Her green eyes were wet, and when she smiled at me I felt warm inside.

The Professor laughed. "You see, it wasn't as hard as you thought."

The young teacher was surrounded by her classmates. Everyone hugged her, saying, "Bravo, you passed your final exam."

I felt good that I attended a 'Practice School' and I knew the name was perfect. I wasn't wishing for a proper partisan name any more.

I headed to the school library to check out the next volume of the Three Musketeers. I couldn't wait to find out if D'Artagnan met the bishop before My Lady arrived.

Over Time:

Professor Ujhelyi was right, I read well. I won prizes in several local and regional reading contests.

The new teaching methods were very effective and the students and the school received numerous awards, including the highest recognition for an institution, called "PIONEERS."

I was amongst the first generation to start school in the nearly finished building. The official name remained "Practice School" until 1994. By then Yugoslavia didn't exist and partisan heroes didn't matter.

Radio: *"The status of a citizen is not determined by a stroke of luck, to be born into a bourgeois family. The working class will accomplish its goals with hard work and dedication to the socialist principles laid down by the Party," said in his speech Momcilo Bozovich, professor of sociology.*

FLY-SHEETS

Late one afternoon I headed home from school wearing my heavy backpack. I clenched my jacket in my hand and balanced a large folder under my arm, containing all of my watercolor paintings. In my other hand was a heavy sack filled with art supplies. I had been comparing art folders with my friends to see which drawings might be good enough to be selected for the competition when suddenly an airplane flew over the school.

I began to run after the plane, shouting to my friends to follow, but they didn't listen. They continued to walk home.

The fly-sheets falling from the plane were still high in the sky. They didn't just fall straight to the ground. I had to run in the direction the wind was carrying this shimmering cloud.

Airplanes often dropped leaflets over the city to

announce events. They would fly low and drop pink, yellow, blue and green papers, each one the size of a large postcard. When the engine noise grew louder, the children would run to the streets and chase the slowly descending fly-sheets. It was a contest to see who could collect the most. At the same time the adults would turn on their radios to listen to the announcements. People who were not near a radio would ask others what was going on.

There was a large grassy area between the houses, and on this day the sky above it was filled with patches of floating colors. I ran towards the meadow and so did all the kids from the neighborhood. A box of aquarelle paint in the sack was hitting my knees.

I spotted a green fly-sheet and I could tell this would be the first to reach the ground. It came down in the usual zigzag pattern. I saw it wouldn't get stuck in a treetop or on a roof.

To free my hands I dropped everything at the side of the rain ditch. The flier drifted away, and I followed it, running, with my arms stretched in the air, reaching, reaching. The books were bouncing in the backpack, the bag pulled on my shoulders. The wind picked up the flier and it flew up instead of down.

My eyes focused on the green sheet of paper. I stretched my arms to the sky and finally, it was almost at my fingertips.

A hand grabbed it in front of my eyes. A boy who was a head taller than me jumped up and snatched it. I lowered my arms, and tears began flooding my eyes. He didn't have a backpack and could jump higher than me.

He saw my lips quivering and grinned with victory. He

looked at the flyer then threw it at the ground towards me. By that time several other fly-sheets floated down and he jumped in the air catching several at once.

I picked up the green paper and smoothed out the wrinkles. I liked to keep my fly-sheets shiny and crisp. My eyes were still wet when I noticed a scribble on it. I was disappointed to think what a messy flier this was when I spotted a pink one descending.

I dropped my backpack to the ground and began to run. I ran after it but the wind picked it up. By the time I caught it I was half-way through the meadow.

From the nearby Tesla residential high-rises, kids rushed to the meadow grabbing the fly-sheets. There were plenty for everyone.

By now more and more fluttered down and I ran to catch yellow and blue ones. I liked to have one of each color and was looking for a green one, since the first one was wrinkled. There were too many kids in the meadow, the wind lifted up the papers and suddenly I was too tired to run.

I picked up my belongings and headed home. I held my cherished fliers in my hand, my eyes still searching for more. Sometimes they landed in yards under the bushes.

On the sidewalk a man walked briskly with a loaf of bread in his hand. "Give me one of the fliers. Let me see what's going on."

I had only one from each color. Which one should I give up? I didn't want to give him any. When adults asked for something, I obeyed because it was part of my pioneer promise and mother told me to be polite with everyone. I thought I would give him the wrinkled, messy one. But he didn't have any fliers so I gave him my nicest, the shiny pink one.

He looked at it and said, "What's this? Now they're sending advertisements from the sky? Ah-ah, mother..."

He looked at me, biting his lip. I knew the word he was not supposed to say in front of kids.

"Are they all the same?" He asked.

I held on tight to the rest of my fly-sheets. I let him look but wouldn't give him another one. I didn't even read what it was about; I didn't care. He shook his head, mumbling as he left. I put the rest of the fliers in my art folder.

A few minutes later a woman carrying two large grocery bags came opposite me and asked, "Did you catch a flier? What are they about this time?"

"Some advertisements," I replied. I wasn't going to give away any more. I wondered if she would put her bags down and ask me for a flier.

She stopped, panting, but held the bags. "What are they advertising now? Another parade? Aye-aye....yet they can't spray the mosquitoes because the airplane fuel is scarce. People can't sit outside."

She shook her head and continued down the sidewalk still talking.

I checked if my fliers were straight in my folder. I was in a hurry to get home before I met anyone else who wanted one of my fly-sheets.

It was dusk already. My knee was bruised and my shoulders were aching from running with my backpack.

When I turned onto our street all the neighbors were outside talking. Mother asked me "Esztikem, did you catch any fliers?"

"I have all the colors except pink."

When I showed her the wrinkled green one she started to shout, "She got one! She got one!"

Everyone looked at it, then laughed happily. The neighbor who worked in the Aurometal clock factory checked it too, and nodded, "Yeah, that's the one. That's the director's signature."

"Where did you catch it?" asked Auntie Confectionery. Her white apron was near my face and smelled like sugar.

I told them and added, "It was very crowded in the meadow. Older boys ran in from far away. They're not from our school."

Mother told me, "The radio announced that five fliers have a factory stamp and a signature. They will drop two over our town and three over Novi Sad. Whoever finds these fliers will get a cuckoo clock."

Our town had 100,000 people, Novi Sad had 150,000. I calculated that it means one flier for 50,000 citizens.

We didn't have a cuckoo clock and I thought it was a great prize.

The whole street was full of people. Everyone came out to see what was going on. The neighbors were laughing and shouting, "We have a winner here. Esztike is a winner."

The man from Aurometal said, "The company is trying new marketing and paid to advertise through fly-sheets." Everyone had questions for him. "Are other companies going to do it? Would Fidelinka give away prizes or just throw the pasta down? When would the Pioneer chocolate factory advertise?"

He didn't know. Mother had only one question, "Is this really a free clock or do I have to pay for it?"

He said, "It's free. If you have any problems, let me know."

Mother was still pursing her lips, which meant she hadn't decided if it was true or not. She didn't believe in luck. Her favorite saying was, 'Don't expect a fried pigeon to fly into your mouth. If you want something, work hard and earn it.'

I always gave a flier to Auntie Confectionery and I offered her one. I let her chose and she picked the yellow one. I gave the blue fly-sheet to mother. She didn't care, she held on to the green one.

Two days later we went to the store. Mother was nervous. Before we entered, she bent down to face me. "Don't be disappointed if you don't get a clock. I can't pay for anything. I left my wallet at home."

I had no doubt in my mind that I'd get a clock. I was a winner and I had come to get my prize.

This would be the first time I ever stepped inside this rich store. It was full of gold necklaces, rings with rubies, wristwatches, and alarm clocks. Our alarm clock came from the flea market. It wasn't fancy.

As I walked through the store, I couldn't hear my own footsteps. The floor had beige carpet all the way to the walls. The stores I usually went in had concrete or squeaky wood floors, where my shoes would clunk on the hard surfaces. Mother often said I walked like a marching band.

Everyone smiled at me when mother gave the store

clerk my fly-sheet.

"Yes, this is a genuine signature," said the red-haired lady. She bent down to face me and smiled. "Congratulations."

I was surprised that she had a powdered face and red lipstick. In the stores I went to, the sales ladies' skin had nothing.

She said, "You can choose any of the clocks from this wall."

She pointed at the sidewall, the one you couldn't see from the shop-window. The clocks were smaller than the ones near the window. These clocks didn't have a balcony for the bird, or geraniums, or a tree.

I asked her, "How does the bird say 'cuckoo'?" I knew that some cuckoos chirped differently. I was curious to find out how my bird would sound.

She said, "These don't say anything. But when the pendulum moves, it looks like they're flying."

I didn't know they could make silent cuckoo clocks. My bird wouldn't chirp?

Mother pointed at a clock, "Listen, it says 'tic-toc', and the pendulum is a pretty leaf. See this golden chain? The weights are pine cones." She was very excited.

I liked the shiny chains and the pretty carvings. I asked, "How does the bird fly?"

The red-haired lady set the clock so the cuckoo would move.

The larger bird on the top pointed its beak to the sky while the little one spread its wings, looking down at the oak leaves. Then I asked the lady, "Please, show me which one could fly the furthest." Mother said, "They are all the same, just pick one."

"Each clock is different," I said and stood there waiting.

The clocks chimed, the birds fluttered back and forth and I watched them all. Some had crooked beaks, others only spread one wing and some gazed sideways. The lady got a ladder to wind the clocks near the ceiling. Mother blinked a lot.

I pointed at a clock, "That one. I like the bird with her wings spread wide. She smiles when she flies."

Mother was in a hurry to leave the store. When we were outside, she smiled again. "It was really free. They took the flier and I didn't have to pay."

I held the package tightly, thinking of my little cuckoo bird. She is silent, but she sees everything and she has the strongest wings.

Over Time:

After twenty years the bird stopped moving. The clock, however, told time for ten more years.

Child: Why is the radio not on?
Mother: They went on my nerves with their empty talks. The philosophy and the rights of the working class! I have work to do.

BACK PAGES OF THE REGISTER

In my head I repeated the poem one more time. I was ready to recite 'My Mother's Hen.' I liked the rhymes in it and the title, *Anyam Tyukja*.

But teacher Bozanich had opened to the back pages of the class register. She wrote notes on those pages, not grades.

"What do your parents do and where do they work?" she asked. We had to stand up and answer one at a time.

I said, "Father is a *sofor* in the March 8 Lace factory, mother is a *haziasszony*." She didn't have a problem with the chauffeur but didn't like the 'woman of the house.'

"That's old fashioned," she said. "We call them a homemaker now. They keep up a house. It is a job too. Don't say *lady* or *housewife*, because they're not just a wife."

The mothers of my friends were *haztartasbeli* too, except Otti's, who worked in a shoe factory.

When Zoli said his father was a doctor, the teacher

smiled. "He is a surgeon, more than a doctor." Zoli was shaking his knees. He was upset because his father took away his sketchpad and scolded him for drawing instead of practicing math.

It was Sanyi's turn. He curled his chapped lips, "He is a boss."

"That's not a profession," said the teacher. "What does he do?"

Sanyi shrugged.

"What kind of school did he finish?"

"How should I know? It was before I was born," said Sanyi.

The class chuckled. Teacher Bozanich was biting her lip. "Where does he work?"

Sanyi grinned, "He recently changed jobs. The name of the company is too long to remember." The teacher mentioned a few, but Sanyi acted unsure which one it could be. We giggled when Sanyi got a homework assignment to find out where his father worked.

Everyone knew if their parents worked in factories like Partizan, November 29, Sever, Zorka and others. It was easy to remember.

Gabi stood up to answer. "Mother goes to the City Hall. It's some long Serbian name. I don't know it." He shook his blonde, curly hair, ready to sit down.

The teacher turned to his twin sister Erika, but she didn't know it either.

Teacher Bozanich wouldn't let Gabi sit down. "Does your mother have to draw or use the ruler?"

Gabi said, "No."

"It's not urban planning. Does she calculate?" the

teacher asked.

He shook his head "no" and the answer was the same for all the other questions.

"What does she say about her work when she gets home?"

"That she is tired," said Gabi quietly.

"She never says anything about her job?" insisted the teacher.

"No."

"I can't think of any other branches at the City Hall." She wrote down 'government office' and Gabi sat down letting out a deep sigh. He didn't get homework like Sanyi.

The teacher liked to ask these questions and I liked to hear new things about my classmates. I knew a lot about my parents but didn't know anything about other parents. I just wished this happened during math class, so we wouldn't have to solve word problems about trains going at different speeds.

We had five minutes before the bell rang. For homework we had to write ten sentences about our parents' jobs. We didn't recite the poem.

The teacher filled in a square at the back of the register. This *Naplo* was a diary about our class. The thick burgundy book was three times the size of my textbook. The front pages had small squares where she wrote down what we learned and what the homework was. The middle section had our grades. The back pages recorded parents' meetings and notes. She said it was 'statistics, and numbers for administrators.' I didn't know what statistics meant but I only cared about the page where my name was and my grades.

When I told mother what we did in school, she frowned. "They know that already, when I signed you up for school I told them. Why do they want this in 2nd grade? Did they think I got a diploma since then?"

I explained to mother that she was not a housewife but a homemaker because we lived in a modern world.

She laughed, "What? I got a new job this year? Wait until your father hears this."

Mother peeled the potatoes and mumbled to herself. "This is hairsplitting, nothing is as good as it was before."

I wanted to recite My Mother's Hen but mother didn't notice me. When she was thinking this deeply, she was far away. I went to play outside.

One day we read a story about a child shoveling coal and going to sleep hungry. The teacher asked, "When you go home from school, who is at home? What do you do and what do you eat?"

Many hands were up and we shouted all at once. "Potatoes, pork chops, eggs, stuffed cabbage." She wanted to hear us one at the time. When we talked she opened the register at the back and took notes. I began to list my favorite foods, imagining the flavors when she stopped me. "I know, your mother is home, she cooks every day." I was sorry I couldn't talk about all the wonderful meals I had.

Then she called the kids who didn't raise their hands.

She said the school had a new cafeteria. We could buy snacks if parents didn't have time to prepare them.

I raised my hand, "Mother says homemade is better, that this is just some wishy-washy food."

Teacher Bozanich's face turned red. "The upstairs students from the teacher training eat there. Sometimes I take it home too. It's good."

I didn't know what to think about the cafeteria. I'd have to try it to find out who was right.

When Tomi said his grandmother opens the door for him, the teacher asked, "Does she live with you?"

"In the evening she goes home to her house. It's five minutes from us."

The teacher knew Tomi lived in a two room flat on the second floor, near the E5. She asked, "Do you play alone outside?"

"Sometimes. Or with other kids from nearby buildings. But I'm not supposed to play where the garages are. Mom has to see me from the window."

"Do you eat hot meals?"

"Granny cooks for the family. My parents eat when they get home at three o'clock."

"Were you ever alone at home?" asked the teacher.

Tomi wrinkled his forehead. "Granny was making plum jam and didn't have enough cellophane. She had some at her house and told me to go with her but I didn't want to. I said I had homework. When she left I watched TV, picked some hawthorn berries."

"Was the jam cooking?"

"No. It was in the oven. When she returned, she was short of breath, all sweaty. She said the cellophane from last year crumbled, she went to several stores but they were all out. Finally she found some near the Majsai bridge. It was a small store behind the lumber yard."

"Do you have a balcony?"

"No, just a window. Mom said I shouldn't open it. But I could pull up the chair and reach the latch. The tree is close, I could reach the branches and pull them closer to me."

Living near a treetop sounded interesting. Tomi's home was very different from mine and I was glad to hear about the grandmother's adventure with the cellophane. My mother never had enough cellophane either when she made the winter compotes. Cellophane was hard to cut and tore easily. If it wasn't tight, mold grew on the compote in two months.

When the bell rang the teacher called some names. The kids stood around her table, Tomi among them. She wanted to talk to their parents.

At home mother asked what happened in school. I told her we didn't learn anything from a textbook, just talked about what we ate at home. Her eyes widened and she was silent. I told her what my friends ate then added, "Gabi has noodles with grits twice a week. Edit likes jam on her pasta."

Mother shook her head. "They want to know everything. What did you say?"

"Sausages, chicken thighs, sauerkraut, stuffed cabbage, ham, prosciutto, meat patties, cakes. Father brings us chocolate from a trip. She wouldn't let me finish."

Mother clasped her hands. "Your teacher thinks we have meat every day. The ham is only at Easter."

"She asked what you cook. She didn't say daily."

"The teacher was asking what you eat on weekdays, most of the time, not holidays. We have meat twice a week plus the roast chicken on Sundays. I cook a lot of vegetables, stuffed squash, green beans, and peas. Did you tell that?"

"I couldn't finish my list but I said peas."

"We can't afford that much meat. Now she thinks how rich we are." She puckered her lips. "Maybe I should talk to her."

"No. I told the truth," I protested.

She shook her head then checked the soup.

"Can I have noodles with grits?" I asked.

She chuckled. "I'm not sure how to make it. When I was a child, Mama made big bowls for us."

"Gabi knows. Put lard in a saucepan, add grits and sugar, mix with noodles."

Mother said, "Instead of sugar it should be bacon bits, or ground meat."

"The teacher also asked Gabi about the meat. He said, sometimes it's cracklings but he likes it better with sugar."

Mother was stirring the soup.

"Could I eat the 9 o'clock snack in the cafeteria? The teacher said it's good."

"Did she say I would have to pay for some lousy meal in a government kitchen?" She slammed the lid on the pot.

"No. Are you angry at me?" I asked.

"No. I'm not in a good mood."

"Why are you angry?"

"I'm mad at this kohlrabi. It's too woody and doesn't have a good flavor. Go and play outside."

Mother got really mad when somebody cheated her at the market. She always wanted first class produce and meat for her family. But when it came to kohlrabi, I didn't care how fresh it was, whether it was boiled or fried. It tasted awful. In class nobody mentioned eating it.

Next week Tomi told me they had to keep the blinds closed for two days because his mother was on sick leave. "They had a big hoopla at home because of the cellophane. Granny cried, dad was hitting the table with his fist, mom got a migraine." Tomi said he wished he didn't bring it up. I was sorry thinking about him in a dark room.

At home I was on my swing and wondered why mother never liked hearing that we just talked in class. I'd tell her where to get cellophane next time she ran out.

Over Time:

When father spoke of the government mother often warned him, "Psst! Not in front of the children."

He laughed, "I don't care. Bandits, and they know it." But I never had to repeat father's words in school.

It was easy when I could answer any question and tell the truth. Later it got more difficult when I had to think of what to say so I wouldn't get in trouble.

Radio: *Our reporters were at the Vegetable Market and asked the small farmers about the new concrete stands. This is what Mari, a resident of Hajdukovo said,*

"Yes, you could wash the stand, it's clean but not good. Too narrow. Not enough space to put the onions in front, now the shoppers could reach over to pick up the delicate goods. They shouldn't handle the tomatoes. They squish the life out of them. No, I pick it in order, small and big, all are good, all for sale. The city Dames just want the large tomatoes. Can't do that. Nobody lets the shoppers pick what they want. And that's the right way."

BEANS AND CRIMSON RED NAILS

I watched the teacher's crimson red nails tapping the white beans. My hand shot up in the air before she finished the question. I wanted to know what would happen to these three large beans.

We were learning how plants grow under different conditions. Teacher Bozanich showed us a picture book and explained that plants grow best in black soil. Plants don't grow too well when the black soil is mixed with sand but the worst is the clay type soil. Plants don't like clay.

"We will prove this." She looked around. "Who would like to do an experiment?"

She gave the first bean to Marti, then offered the second one to Magdi. Magdi laughed. "I can't grow any plants. When I water the houseplants they die."

"Try it," said the teacher.

I raised my arm even higher and begged, "Pleeease, I want to plant one. Can I get a bean, please?"

She handed me the third bean. I held it in my palm like a treasure. She assigned the kind of soil we were to prepare at home and gave us instructions on how to care for the plant.

Marti had to grow the bean in black soil, I got the mixture of black soil and sand, and Magdi got the clay.

Magdi laughed. "My bean will probably wilt before the homework is due."

When I got home I ran through the house, shouting, "Look what I have." I opened the door to the basement.

Mother was dragging a bag of cement from one corner to the other. She mumbled to herself. "He and his building mania and remodeling. He should have been a construction worker, not a chauffeur."

I yelled, "Give me a jar now. I have to plant." I ran to the pantry where two shelves were full of empty jars.

"That's for pickles, don't touch it." Mother was behind me. I didn't know anyone could get up from the basement this fast.

Anything I wanted was for a jam or compote. "You can't put dirt in these," she said.

"I plant it in water," I explained.

"What kind of bean is this? Nothing grows without soil."

She gave me a round bottle but I didn't like it. I grabbed a tall jar. "This is the one from the book. I'm doing an experiment. After I'm done you can use it to put peaches in."

"An experiment? This was in the book?" She sighed, "All right, even if you put dirt in it, before I use them I have to boil the bottles anyway."

I filled the jar one third with water then put the bean in it.

"You could plant it in the soil right away. Do you think the farmers dilly-dally with each bean like this? They throw a fistful of seeds in a little ditch, cover it with dirt and water it."

"If you sprout it, it grows faster." I tried to defend my bean, reading my notes.

"I don't know what they teach you but this is not the future." Mother was convinced everyone would starve if the farmers began to use this new method.

When the bean sprouted five days later, I prepared the soil.

First I went to the basement where we kept a tub of sand. I measured it then removed the dry geranium leaves, which had fallen off the bunch hanging from the ceiling. The dry leaves crumbled, making my hands smell sweet. The geraniums 'wintered out' here and in spring, the sticks with roots were planted in the yard. I hurried up, almost knocking over a bundle of oleanders.

I dug up black dirt from our garden. The soil felt soft, unlike the grains of sand. I had two equal mounds. I mixed them and planted the bean. Then I dumped a cup of water on it, which splattered dirt on the tablecloth.

Mother said, "Be gentle so the bean stays covered. The roots must grab the soil."

She was excellent with plants so I listened to her. Our hallway was full of lush green plants even in winter. All my friends' houses had entryways with greenery. Our mothers gave each other cuttings and shared tips about planting.

In two days green shoots appeared. The following days I kept looking at my beautifully sprouting bean. I was curious what shape the leaves would be. The morning the first leaves opened I watched the pointy edges while eating my sausage and tomato sandwich for breakfast. I liked the many shades and patterns of green. By the time I put on my shoes the leaves were bigger.

My bean was growing fast. I turned it around so all the leaves would get equal light. It was getting tall.

Mother warned me, "Leave it alone before you break off the stalks."

The day before I had to take my lush plant to school I was in the kitchen counting the leaves. The classical violin concert ended on the radio.

Radio: *The Tanjug reports from the United States – On June 5th senator Robert Kennedy was shot with a revolver in the kitchen of Hotel Ambassador in Los Angeles. He died on June 6th.*

I didn't know who Robert was, but he had to be important if Tanjug mentioned him. We got all the international information from our Tanjug news agency which had offices worldwide. I wondered about a place where people could buy guns and shoot others in a kitchen. I knew America was the wild west where they carried revolvers but that was hundreds of years ago. In our country only the military had guns to protect us in the case of war.

Radio: *We continue with agricultural news. The aphids attacked the orchards causing serious damage and the director of Vocara stated they won't be able to meet the planned production quantity. "People won't be drinking peach juice next winter and our export will be down," he declared then asked the government leadership to take appropriate steps to exterminate the pests in order to avoid future destruction to the crop.*

Frantically, I checked the leaves on my plant when mother's voice startled me. "Leave it!"

She was behind me.

"What if the aphids attack my bean?"

She waved her hand, "There are no aphids in this house. Go and play outside."

Next day I carried my clay pot triumphantly. The leaves reached my face and I had trouble seeing in front of me.

When we lined up the bean plants, mine was almost twice as tall as the one grown in black soil. The teacher was really annoyed that the second plant was so lush and huge. She asked me, "Did you follow the directions? Did you use sand?"

I poked my finger in the dirt and showed her the layers

of light brown sand among the black dirt. "We have very good black soil in our yard. Mother grows lots of vegetables."

She pointed her rose red nails at my plant. "How many times did you water it?" Her lipstick was rose red too.

I pulled out my notes and I read the log, but she was shaking her head. She didn't believe me and I couldn't understand why. She questioned Marti, who planted in black soil, "Where did you keep the plant?"

"On the window sill, it had plenty of light. And I watered it regularly," she replied. The teacher got more annoyed.

She was happy only when she looked at the bean-stalk grown in clay. That was the smallest plant. Magdi laughed, "I'm happy the plant is alive. It's small, but I didn't ruin it."

The teacher smiled at her and showed the class the little bean stalk. She turned towards the other two plants and said with annoyance, "Take them away from my desk. You're going to get Plus for extra work."

I whispered to Marti, "How come our bean stalks made her angry?"

"I don't know." She shrugged and turned to her next assignment in the book.

I carried my plant home wondering why it didn't get praised. What did I do wrong? Now the plant didn't look good to me.

When I got home mother was raking the soil in the flower garden. Her fingernails were black with dirt. I gave her the plant and when she spoke her voice was softer than usual. "Did they like your bean stalk?"

I shrugged.

"Do you want to transplant it into the ground? This would be a good place for it. The vines would climb on the pole," said mother.

I was so surprised that mother was offering my bean a place in her flower garden. This was the front yard. It was full of roses and pretty flowers so people from the street could admire them. Vegetables were allowed to grow only on the side of the house.

I planted my bean next to the roses and lilies. Mother trimmed back the lower branches of the rosebush so my plant would get more sunshine. She even cut off a stem of lily and I put it in a vase. She never cut off her flowers. She said they last longer in the garden.

From my room I could watch my beautiful bean. Each day it was climbing the pole higher.

Over Time:

Magdi went on to get a degree in Horticulture. She owned a flower shop, and named her daughter Margareta which means Daisy. Then she had an orchard. One year a freeze wiped out all her trees. Now she paints landscapes.

Marti has lots of house plants but prefers green grass in her yard. All her plants are very lush since they grow in black soil.

I moved to California and my home is on two acres of rocky soil. The eucalyptus trees thrive in my yard on their own. Anything I try to grow shrivels up.

Radio: *The Collective Farming annual report states that 25% of their land is not suitable for industrial agriculture. Last year 9% of their parcels remained unseeded and another 16% had a poor yield of wheat, sunflower and corn. Therefore the* Zadruga, *with the leadership of the Communist Party, proposed the selling of unused land to small farmers who could cultivate the land by hand or small machinery and plant various produce. The referendum would allow farmers to sell surplus crop to canning factories.*

In the villages now 60% of the households have electricity, reported the Bureau of People's Living Standards. They proposed to evaluate the socio-economic structure of the villages and the reasons why Party membership is low in agricultural regions.

Child: What are they talking about?
Mother: The land belongs to the farmers who cultivate it with love.
Child: Doesn't the *Zadruga* love their land?
Mother: Go and do your thing now. I'll call you when they start the children's program.
Child: Will you listen to *Miklos bacsi's* folktales too?

MASKED BALL

I circled the Gypsy Baron and Baroness for the best

costume, best dancers, and best performance categories. My cousin Jolcsi was the Gypsy Baroness. Her satin dress had yellow, red and purple ruffles and she danced playing the tambourine. Ribbons flowed in her dark hair and she wore a sparkling mask covering half of her face.

The stage was full of dancing couples, dressed as shepherds, princesses, and hunters. I didn't know who Jolcsi would be in the masked ball. She kept it a secret from us but I recognized her long legs and slender fingers. Why did she dance barefoot if she was a baroness?

Cousin Jolcsi was in eighth grade and her brother Vili finished all his schools. I had begun third grade and this was the first time I had attended a ball.

I wore a black velvet mask over my eyes, just like in the operas I saw on TV. I took it off when I was eating because I couldn't see the pork chops properly. When I cut the meat, the French fries slid off my plate.

With the small spoon I carefully ate the compote. For this festive occasion mother had stitched a lace collar onto my velour dress and I didn't want the juice to drip on it. On Monday mother would take off the collar so it would become a regular dress for school.

My parents, Gizi and I sat at the table with Jolcsi's parents who were also my Godparents. They lived 85 kilometers away from us, in a village called Ada. I always enjoyed visiting them.

Godmother whispered to my mother. "They practiced for months and also learned waltzes and tango. All the girls had chaperones, just like in old times. We, the *gardedames*, sat by the wall and watched them."

Mother raised her eyebrows. "They do this in school?"

"No," replied Godmother, "this is a separate dance club. But they let them use the community hall. I don't know how they got the permit, but they did."

In Subotica we had folk dance groups and sports clubs but no ballroom dancing. In school we were taught that the bourgeoisie spent their time at balls and banquets. They led a decadent lifestyle and exploited the peasants. Luckily, that was the past and we now had new rules.

This hall was decorated with colorful crepe paper, and the ribbons hung off the ceiling and walls. It had a wooden floor but wasn't shiny like in the movies and we didn't have candles.

After dinner Godfather mingled and seemed like he knew everybody. A skinny man gave him a bundle wrapped in newspaper. A woman gesticulated angrily but the men laughed. Godfather put the package in his pocket and moved on.

When the musician set up his dulcimer, everyone clapped. Then a violinist, an accordion player and a man with a double bass came in and they played a waltz. My cousin and her costumed classmates danced on the stage.

At the end of the dance my mother turned to my Godmother. "This is like the first ball, back then."

Couples from the tables walked to the middle of the hall and began to waltz.

Godmother nodded, "This is the best band on this side of river Tisza. They promised to play at Vili's wedding."

She poked my father. "Brother, go and dance."

He smiled. "I'm not good at it. I would rather watch them."

I stood up. "Apu, dance with me."

Father laughed then finally walked me to the empty space between the tables. When I grabbed his hands he kept repeating. "I'm not good at this."

I saw waltzing on TV and I danced with my sister but this was a real ball. I stepped left then right and watched the people nearby to see how they did it.

When I moved to one side, father moved the opposite way, and we were pulling each other like we were wrestling. Then he stood in one place, shifting his weight from the left to right foot while I skipped on my own. Then he spun me around and I was thrilled. That was a real dance. I was spinning and he held my hand. When I got dizzy, he hugged me and led me back to the table.

Then Gizi jumped in front of him. "My turn." And pulled him to the crowd. A minute later she stumbled back to the table, giggling and holding onto father.

My head cleared up, I was ready for my next dance when mother stood up. "It's my turn." Father held her hand and they walked to the dance floor. He knew how to waltz with mother. Her eyes sparkled when he spun her around. Then they continued with the tango.

"I want to dance again," said Gizi, and she began whirling towards father.

Godmother called her back. "Would you like another cake? Or a strudel?"

"Cake," replied Gizi and sat down at lightning speed.

We got a second serving of dessert when Godfather returned to our table.

I was enjoying my plum strudel and looked at my Godfather's large hand. I knew he scrubbed them before the ball but his fingers and fingernails were still black with oil stains. We were almost late arriving because Godmother sent him back to the bathroom to wash up again. He made machine parts in his own shop and worked from dawn until late into the night.

From his pocket he pulled out a metal part, wrapped in newspaper then studied it carefully. "The John Deere tractor is kaput and I must fix this cylinder. Or make a new one."

Godmother nudged him to put it away. "We're not leaving. Enjoy the music."

"I paid for the band but it doesn't mean I should sit here all night," said Godfather. "The Kirics farm can't wait, they have to plow the fields."

The Gypsy Baron and Baroness walked by our table. Jolcsi looked away. She told me before she would be *incognito* all night. I wished she would hug me but she went to dance with the Baron.

Looking at his daughter, a smile flooded Godfather's face. He put the cylinder in his pocket and pulled his chair closer to Godmother's.

At the end of the ball the Gypsy Baron and Baroness got first prize and an envelope.

Afterwards we took the train home. Gizi was asleep in mother's arms. I wondered when would I dance again and if we would be able to organize a ball at home. Where would you get a band in the town? Would the ball be real without a band?

The steam engine whistled and I fell asleep on father's lap as the train was chugging through the night.

Over Time:

In third grade some of my friends got record players and we began to dance at birthday parties. Whoever had a record player offered to bring it along.

In high school it became a tradition to waltz to the 'Blue Danube' at New Year's Eve celebrations.

Next time I attended a masked ball I was in college.

Radio: *Discipline is a key factor in achieving results but harsh punishments bring out resistance in the young.*

MODERN METHODS

The classroom was unusually quiet as teacher Bozanich finished reading a story.

She said, "Before the war, when this country was a kingdom, the teachers and parents beat the children to discipline them. The teachers hit them with a stick; their parents used a belt."

In the story the students were punished when they didn't sit up straight or didn't learn a poem.

Teacher Bozanich looked at us. "We have a modern education system. The Pioneer Union sets the rules and the teachers can't use physical punishment. They believe it's a primitive way to educate the young. How do your parents punish you? And what did you do?"

It was normal for most kids to get an occasional spanking. We didn't talk about it because it would have been embarrassing to admit. But now the whole class shouted at once. "Spanking," or "My bum." Then other answers: "smack in my face, belt, pulling my ear, slapping, I run and she chases me."

We giggled at the end and asked. "What's the right way to punish kids?"

She shrugged. "The pedagogues are working on a plan. One example would be standing in the corner."

That sounded embarrassing. Everyone would know you were bad.

Teacher Bozanich showed us a booklet and said, "This is one of the international organizations for children, called UNICEF. Soon after WWII, Yugoslavia was one of the first countries to work with them."

There was a drawing of the globe with children around it holding hands. The colors of the kids were yellow, white, brown, black, and reddish. They wore folk costumes. One of them had a straw skirt. I was surprised to see that not all girls wore ribbons, that some had hats, others had flowers or sticks in their hair.

We asked, "What does UNICEF do? Are we going to visit these kids? How could we talk to them if they don't know Hungarian?"

Teacher Bozanich said, "The Pioneer Union has programs but I don't know what kind. UNICEF makes sure all children go to school because in some countries they work from an early age. You'll learn this in upper classes."

I was a little disappointed because I wanted to meet those children, especially the reddish one with feathers in her hair.

The teacher was more interested in why we got spanked at home. We had to answer one-by-one and sometimes she took quick notes.

"Father slapped me once but my brother got spanked

with a belt," said Edit. "He had talked back saying father was wrong."

Magdi giggled. "My sister dropped mother's lipstick in the toilet then said she didn't touch it. Mother slapped her."

This couldn't happen to me because my mother didn't have a lipstick.

The teacher said, "Lying is very bad. You promised to be honest, remember that."

Otti said, "Mama spanked me because I ate candy before dinner. When I couldn't eat the peas, she asked if I had sweets and I said I didn't. Then she saw the missing candy."

"Mother spanked me when I pushed my sister and pulled her hair," I said. "Once she slapped me because I told her she couldn't cook."

Zoli grinned, "I kicked the ball into the neighbor's garden. I tried to be careful but that ball always flies the wrong way. Dad took off his belt and his pants fell down." He shook his head.

Teacher Bozanich just listened.

Next time mother came home from a parent conference her face was all frowns when she talked to father. "We had a lecture on how to discipline children. They told us, no spanking." She glanced at me. "I only know that parents spank their children. I never heard about these modern methods."

Father raised his eyebrows. "Then how do you punish them?"

Mother shrugged. "It was vague. They'll publish something for the teachers so they can tell us next time.

This will continue."

Father said, "They really care about the children." He gazed at the rug. "My father told me to pick out the belt, take off my pants, and then he gave me a beating. He didn't want to ruin the one pair of pants I had."

I remembered the stories about how his stepmother complained about the boys fighting over spoons. Four boys ate out of one pot. They had two big spoons and two small ones. Whoever got the small spoons ended up hungry. They also got in trouble for stealing bacon or eating raw eggs. That's why in our house the pantry was bigger than the bathroom.

Mother said, "The Pioneer Union, Teachers Board, Education Ministry, everyone is working on reforms. We'll have a world-class school system." She looked at me. "What did you tell the teacher?"

I shrugged. "That sometimes you spank us."

She shook her head. "That's true. I have a quick temper. I didn't hurt you. Did I?"

I shrugged. "A little. Sometimes."

Father looked at mother. "Discipline is important. But they're right. There are other ways."

Mother stared at the rug.

I had homework so I went to the bedroom where Gizi played with her doll. She was much calmer when *Apu* was home. If she wanted to wrestle with him, she had to behave.

The glass door was closed but I could hear my parents talking.

"These are new times. We can't do everything the same way we were raised," said father.

Mother's voice sounded like she had just cried. "When I'm waiting for you for endless hours I don't always have the patience for them. My hand is quick but I don't hurt them."

Father pondered. "One is school age the other wants to play. Four years is a big difference." He chuckled. "I often played tricks on my brothers, and they didn't like it."

Mother whispered and I opened the glass door to hear better. "These two constantly bicker. I tried to leave them alone to figure things out for themselves but they never tire. They yell and scream like they're being skinned alive."

"I know how boys fight," said father, "but I don't know about girls."

"Since she learned to read, Eszti can't put her books down," said mother. "Gizi lost her playmate. She used to wait for Eszti to finish her homework. Now she reads and the little one wants to roughhouse. Both holler for me. 'Eszti won't play with me,' or 'Gizi poked me.' Every day is like that, the whole month. The neighbors can hear them. What will they say? That I stay home and can't raise my children?"

She shouted to me. "Don't eavesdrop, close that door." *Anyu* always had an eye on me, I knew I couldn't hide from her.

I still heard them through the glass door. She turned to father, "Imagine, there is an organization called UNICEF helping kids all over the world get an education."

His voice was raspy. "Who could have thought that one day organizations exist to protect the children! Not like in our time when they sent us to serve, right after we learned to read and count."

Mother sniffled. "I practiced the alphabet, drawing letters in the dirt while watching the geese. My stepfather said, 'You're a girl. Why would you need school? Cleaning is good enough for you.' "

He said, "Whatever they say about Tito, he is for progress. We're part of the modern world. Did they give any advice about punishments?"

"Yes," she said. "Talk to them first. Make them clean or do work they normally wouldn't. Also keep them busy. When they learn or play they don't have time to misbehave."

Father shook his head. "UNICEF, eh? Worldwide."

Mother whispered. "When I was leaving I heard two mothers telling the teacher they wished their husbands heard this because they're quick to use the belt. One of them is a doctor, the other is a factory director, educated men. One mother lamented that she doesn't know how to stop him. He seems backward-thinking when it comes to children and obedience. He thinks their home is an army barrack. The teacher said to bring him to the next parent meeting or just come in any time. She will explain to him how this directive is coming from above."

He said, "Often they bring my blood to a boil with their politics, but they're good to the children."

They talked but I couldn't hear them so I finished my homework. It was interesting to have heard what they thought about my school.

The door opened and mother motioned towards the living room. "Apu wants to talk to you."

Both Gizi and I stood in front of him. On rare occasions

when father 'talked' to us, he would say two or three sentences.

Father leaned back in the armchair and looked at us for a while. "Sit down."

We sat on the divan.

"What's the quarrel about?"

Gizi whined. "She doesn't want to play with me."

I said, "When I'm reading she jumps on me yelling 'Wrestle, come on, throw me on the ground.' She almost tore a page out of my book."

Father said, "Don't quarrel, you're sisters. Come to an agreement nicely. If mother tells you to stop fighting then listen. Otherwise she must punish you. Is that clear?"

"Yes," we replied.

"Gizi, don't nag your sister. She is a schoolgirl now. She has tasks she must do and things she likes to do. You have to learn to play alone."

She shook her head. "But I'm bored."

Father raised his voice. "I had one wooden toy soldier yet I didn't know what boredom was. What's in that basket? Don't just toss your toys in there and say you don't know what to do. If you don't play with them I'll take the basket up to the attic. Clear?"

Gizi sniffled, nodding.

Mother gesticulated with her hands, agreeing with father. I was glad Gizi was told to leave me alone.

Father turned to me. "Eszti, you're a big girl now and it's good that you like to read. You do your homework and become smarter every day. But you are still a child and you should play. The books will wait for you. You have your whole life to read. But you have only this time to be a child and play. Clear?"

I was thinking that often I didn't know what to do with my sister. She just wanted to wrestle.

"You don't always have to play with your sister," said father. I was amazed that he could read my mind. "Make up games you like."

I said "yes" while mother raised her eyebrows and pointed her chin towards *Apu* which meant 'You heard your father.'

He never talked this long about our behavior. He stood up, relieved. "What if I lay bricks under the swing so you could use it now?"

Gizi and I cheered and hugged father. Each fall he took down the swing because the ground was muddy underneath. In late spring he put it back but we couldn't use it after heavy rains.

When he gently stroked my head with his strong hand, warmth flowed down my back.

Over Time:

I invented games I liked to play and my sister happily went along.

Even now I enjoy making up games.

Radio: *We must ensure that capitalism and the bourgeois class will never gain power to bring us down. Together we can protect the country from radicals and reactionists. Above all, we must protect brotherhood and unity.*

Child: Anyu, what are they saying?
Mother: It's good that you could go to Hungarian school. You understand everything better and learn more in your native tongue.

A VISITOR

I listened but couldn't understand what teacher Bozanich was talking about. She held up the book, pointed at the dancers and spoke about equality and unity just like the radio announcer. I was curious why the girls wore gold coins in their hair instead of ribbons but I didn't want to raise my hand.

A single guest sat in the back of the class, under Tito's picture.

Teacher Bozanich was dressed in a white blouse and a blue skirt which she wore for the Republic Day celebration. Her silk scarf was tied into a fashionable bow. The color matched her deep red lipstick.

Yesterday she said, "We'll have a visitor from another school, observing and learning how we teach here so they can use our methods elsewhere."

Our school was famous. We learned math using color sticks and we often had to show how they worked. When pedagogues visited, Professor Ujhelyi brought them to our class. They smiled and asked questions. I felt special because many people were interested in our notebooks.

This visitor came in for the Knowledge of Nature and Society class. She looked old, her wrinkled face had no powder. She carried a leather bound notepad and her nylon stockings were twisted around her legs. Usually the third class stockings did that, the ones Slovenians wouldn't buy from father's factory.

She never smiled. The visitor probably learned a lot from our teacher because she wrote down every word. I wondered why she didn't know that at the end of WWII most people in Yugoslavia couldn't read and write, and that Tito and the Party built schools. I heard about it on the radio.

Teacher Bozanich always explained everything well, but that day she talked in a strange voice and added words that made learning difficult. For homework we had to write ten sentences about what brotherhood and unity meant in our neighborhood. I was worried how I would do my homework.

After class teacher Bozanich invited the brown clothed visitor for a cup of coffee in the lounge but she pursed her wrinkled lips and said, "No."

My teacher asked, "Would you like to see the children's notebooks?"

The visitor shook her head 'No' and added, "I'll send in my report, then you'll hear back. In two or three weeks."

"Could I see it before you send it in?" asked teacher Bozanich.

"No. Good Bye."

I felt sorry for my teacher. In our school everyone smiled and that made it a good place. Now I felt a knot in my stomach because I didn't know how to do my homework.

During the next class teacher Bozanich explained, "Show what your neighbors cook, and tell how they speak a different language but laugh together, and so on."

We asked, "Which school did the visitor come from?" We felt sorry for the kids who had a teacher like her.

"She is in administration." Teacher Bozanich waved her hand in annoyance. Administrators, just like statistics, had nothing to do with my grades so I didn't care.

She began to explain how the Duna and Tisza rivers shaped our region. I opened my textbook and listened to her, mesmerized. With my finger I traced the winding blue river from the Black Forest to the Black Sea.

Over Time:

Throughout the years different people showed up in our class. No matter how kind our teacher was these visitors didn't smile and never looked at our colored math sticks. They didn't come often, and as soon as they left I was glad.

One of teacher Bozanich's colleagues said, "I remember she was always afraid. Her husband was a member of the Communist Party and she was under a lot of pressure."

Professor of Sociology on Radio: *Religion takes away the power from the people. To raise the consciousness of the working class we need to give them the opportunity to build a life for themselves, with their own hands, minds and willpower. It's not God that decides one's destiny, it's man himself.*

Mother pounded the meat louder then turned off the radio.

THE GRAY EYES

At age eleven I had to examine my life. I was preparing for my first confession. I didn't know if I had sinned or not and, if I had, I really didn't remember how many times. What am I going to tell the priest if I can't remember? I was really worried.

All my friends were getting ready for confession so I tried to get help from them. "Do you know what you are going to say in the confession booth?" I asked Vali, hoping that I would get ideas about my sins.

She said, "Yeah," but wouldn't give out any details. This was the first time we didn't share our thoughts. It was strange that I was on my own to figure this out. Maybe I could find a book to help me.

Thursday afternoon in the church basement we gathered for another Faith Class. The old and balding Father Wurtz sat there with eyes closed, quietly praying in Latin. When he finished he leafed through the Bible. He was always slow to start talking, giving us a chance to quiet down and feel sacred.

I was eager to find out more about sins. "Where could we buy a Bible?" I asked.

"The church prints enough to give them to the priests. We're not allowed to sell them and you can't buy them in bookstores. The government doesn't print them," he replied.

Magdi fidgeted. "Granny has a leather book with a cross on it. Not sure what it is. Doesn't have the hammer and sickle." She giggled.

"How could anyone own a Bible if you can't buy it?" We asked.

Father Wurtz sighed. "If they saved it from old times, before the war. Ask your grandparents or any old relatives."

Then he explained the Ten Commandments in a monotone voice and added, "If something is not clear, ask about it." He clasped his hands ready to pray.

He seemed surprised when we asked a lot of questions. I was all ears, trying to understand if I had committed any cardinal sins. On judgment day I sure didn't want to stand on the left side of Jesus, going to hell because I didn't pay attention to the priest.

I didn't understand the 6th commandment. I asked "What does it mean to fornicate?"

He looked away, coughed and smiled at the same time.

He said, "It's when people do things outside of marriage. Like a man is looking at women on the streets, or watching the neighbor's wife. Certain things are allowed in marriage but not before." He didn't look at us, he gazed at the cross and sighed.

We stared at him, waiting for more explanation.

He was the only person I knew with light gray eyes. I wondered if that helped him see holy things better.

Then he talked about the sacrament of marriage and what God's intention was. It was still foggy but I thought I understood it.

On the day of the First Confession we lined up and waited quietly. These were my friends but we avoided each other's gaze. I was embarrassed because of my sins. Soon it was my turn. Going into that brown box made my palms sweat.

I saw only the priest's ear and heard a Latin prayer. His hand propped up his forehead, facing away from me.

I started with a trembling voice, "I have sinned and came to confess." Then I took a deep breath and said it loudly, "I committed the cardinal sin of fornication."

Father Wurtz jolted. His gray eyes stared at me furiously. "Shhh, quieter."

I whispered, "I fornicated."

He whispered, "How?"

I said, "I looked at boys."

He waited. "And?"

"I looked at boys twice."

"Anything else?" he whispered, glaring at me.

My mind searched my past. I was thinking, 'Wasn't it enough that I had a cardinal sin? Am I supposed to have minor sins too? Do I need to confess one of each?'

He returned to his original position, his ear turned to me again.

I tried to find another sin when he said, "Do your homework and don't look at boys. Say five prayers of 'Our Father.' "

What a relief! But why was he upset with me?

That was the only cardinal sin I ever had to confess. After that I was too sleepy to say my prayers in the morning so each week I had something to confess. At first I thought I should have a different sin each week but couldn't find any I committed. The priest didn't mind, either. He gave me the absolution and told me to say five prayers of 'Our Father.' I learned that cardinal sins and minor sins carry the same penalty.

Next time I looked at Robi who was smiling at me, I smiled back, enjoying his gaze. Then I remembered I'd have to confess my cardinal sin. We're not married. I remembered the angry gray eyes and I quickly turned my head away.

I soon forgot about the first confession. But from then on, I wasn't looking at boys eye-to-eye.

Over Time:

I was in high school when I finally understood the meaning of the sixth commandment. By that time I wasn't going to weekly confessions. School life was too busy. I was often looking at boys but only secretly, with a quick glance before averting my eyes.

At the time I was finishing college, I was deeply in love with my new boyfriend. One day I ran into an old friend. He told me he got married and that they were ready to have a child.

I blurted out, "Did you know I was so much in love with you the first year of college? It took me a long time to forget you."

He stared at me in shock. "You, too?"

"What do you mean?" I mumbled.

His voice trembled. "After serving in the army I came back looking for you, but you moved and I couldn't find you. I searched for months. I wanted to marry you, I loved you so much."

I felt a knot in my throat. "Why didn't you tell me that five years ago? We danced together that New Year's Eve." I never forgot that waltz and how he held me in his arms.

He replied, "You never looked at me, always turned your head away. I couldn't see your eyes and I thought you didn't care for me."

For the first time I looked into his light gray eyes without fear.

Radio: *Our rapid industrialization raised the standard of living for all citizens. Almost every household has a radio and every five households owns a television set.*

Dear children, we now continue with 'Little pig's adventures.'

WHAT IS KITSCH?

In 3rd grade in Knowledge of Society the teacher was explaining that we should keep our home clean and decorate it with artwork. We shouldn't buy kitsch because that's bad. I didn't know what kitsch was.

At home we had small porcelain figures on our coffee table: a pigeon, a squirrel, a dancing girl in a long dress. My favorite was the candy box. The lid was golden with a blue rim and red flowers. I often picked up the lid with great joy to examine the lacy gold pattern and check what kind of surprise was underneath. Candy or leftover sugar crystals from the previous batch; most often there was no candy. I would stick my finger in and lick the sugar trying to guess which candy had been in there.

Teacher Bozanich asked, "What kind of statues, paintings or other art work do you have in your home?"

I raised my hand and told her about the squirrel and the dancer and added, "Mother doesn't let me dust them, so I won't break them."

The teacher waved her hands dismissively, "That's all kitsch."

Then I remembered the real artwork. "We have a white cloth on the wall next to the stove. It has red embroidery of a young woman with roses and words, 'Where my rose is there my heart is.' Father bought this wall protector at the fair. Mother planted lots of roses and her name is Rose."

Teacher Bozanich said, "That's not art either."

Then I remembered the paintings. "We have little paintings of saints. My Godmother gave me several of them and I kept them in the prayer book."

"No, that isn't art either," said the teacher.

I sat down realizing that we don't have any art at home.

She moved on to another student.

Vali said, "We have a painting of a meadow. It's big and covers the whole wall."

The teacher was excited to hear that and asked who the artist was but Vali didn't know. Vali sighed and pointed to her notebook, "The frame is this wide and collects lots of dust which I have to wipe off every Saturday morning."

Teacher Bozanich said, "Next time look in the corner and read the name."

Vali replied, "The scribble looked like black grass. That person had ugly handwriting."

The teacher was even more enthusiastic, "Ask your mother. It could be a famous artist."

I was surprised that the teacher wasn't upset about the

ugly handwriting. We were told to write nice round letters and if we didn't, she got irritated and we had to rewrite the whole essay. How come an artist could have ugly handwriting?

The writing on our cloth at home was very nice, legible with even letters. But she said that wasn't art. I raised my hand again. "We don't have any of this artwork yet but my mother likes the neighbor's garden decorations. These are little statues of the seven dwarfs. She just couldn't afford to buy any yet. They have red jackets, big red noses and big smiles. I also enjoy looking at the colorful glass balls which are on the top of the sticks that the rose bushes are tied to."

The teacher said, "That's not art, either. Art makes you feel good."

I didn't understand her. The glass balls were shiny and I could see the clouds or sunset in them. I liked to look at the dwarfs, too. They all faced towards the street so everyone could enjoy them. I often stood by the fence and watched the dwarfs. They all smiled at me and made me feel good.

She said, "Art in a home shows refined taste. You should never put kitsch in your house. It's tacky and ugly."

I didn't think she had seen our porcelain squirrel yet. It was a real statue and looked like it was ready to leap for a hazelnut. By the end of the class I still didn't understand what kitsch was. In our home I had pretty things around me. Mother wouldn't put anything ugly in our new brick house. Maybe my teacher could come to see how nice and clean our home is.

Over Time:

In 5th grade the art teacher explained once again what kitsch was. She showed us the popular plastic flowers. "These are not art. The little figurines are not art."

Teacher Kisferenc showed us various objects and pictures from an art book. "This is art. It has a unique carving, this is hand painted and not mass produced in a factory."

Finally I understood that our porcelain figurines were kitsch. But then I looked at the painting of St. George in agony and the bust of Voltaire with his dusty, curly hair. I thought *It doesn't matter what a shiny squirrel is called*. I'd rather have the squirrel smiling from the table than the angry philosopher staring at me.

Radio: *In front of the Primary Court of Subotica a ceremony was held to unveil the statue of the Ballad of the Hanged, by sculptor Nandor Glid. 'The self-consciousness of the brave resists the cruel death' was written on the plaque to commemorate the execution of the communist party members in 1941 by the fascists.*

Child: Anyu, is the war memorial made of gypsum too?
Mother: It's bronze or marble. Gypsum is for vases, garden decorations – or to make a cast for broken bones.

BIG SMILE

At home I talked so much about art that mother decided to make her own garden statue if we could find a pattern for it.

My fairy tale books had nice drawings but most figures were behind a rock or covered by branches. Mother said, "We can't make a statue squatting."

"This one smiles," I pointed to the dwarf which was visible to his shoulders.

When I read the stories, it didn't matter that most drawings were only partially finished. Now we leafed through all my books until we found two complete pictures. One was a troll with a fuzzy hat but his angry face scared me. We picked the other one, the stern looking dwarf, facing sideways.

I traced it onto tissue paper. We thought it would be easy to make him look happy. Using a large piece of paper mother drew parallel lines around my small picture and kept enlarging it.

"Make it bigger. Bigger!" I said until the dwarf's large belly was at the edge of the paper. It was as tall as my little sister, Gizi.

"When are we going to make him smile?" I asked.

"First we'll build a frame. The statue has to be hollow," said mother. She bent the chicken wires different ways but it was always a ball or an egg shape, never a figure. She used pliers to shape the stomach. To make the feet, I twisted the wire. It was square and didn't look like a shoe.

Mother frowned. "We can't do it."

I curved the wire, trying to form a shoe. I said, "Look, I have his nose." His shoe would be covered by dirt anyway but he had to have a nose.

She sighed, "We could make a flat statue."

Then she began a frame by bending a thick wire along the lines on the tissue paper. "It's not right. It won't be like a real one," she said and laid the fine mesh across to create the backing.

I cheered on. "It looks good. Nobody would see the back part." I tried to make his nose smaller but the wire was too tangled. "Our dwarf will be happy and smile all the time. That's the most important."

When the wires scratched mother's hand, she decided that the frame was done.

Then I poured water into a bucket filled with gypsum. White chalk-like powder floated in the air, and when mother bent down to stir the gypsum some of it settled on her black hair. We didn't know if we should leave the tissue paper in the frame or not. After some debate we thought it would make it stronger. Then we poured the thick liquid over the wires.

Mother hesitated. "I'm not sure how to draw his ear when he is facing sideways."

I turned my head. "Easy. Do you see my ear?"

She ran her finger over my cheek. "What about the earlobes? And the inner part?"

I reassured her with a wave of my hand. "We can do it. In school we draw everything. At first I don't know how to do it but when the teacher explains, I can do it."

Before the gypsum dried we carved the dwarf's face using a long nail but the eyes and mouth disappeared as the soft liquid flowed. We agreed to paint his face and clothes after it dried, and it was all right if his jacket didn't have creases on his belly.

This was the first time mother and I made art together and I enjoyed it. The gypsum pulled my skin tight and made me feel artistic. I was sorry when mother told me to wash it off before it becomes hard and looks like plaster on a broken arm.

When the dwarf dried we tried to remove the wire mesh but we couldn't. We painted his jacket red, his eyes blue and his lips red.

"That's not a big smile. I want it bigger," I said.

Mother thought the lips were the right size. She pondered how to draw the right ear.

While she put an extra layer of paint on the belly where the wires showed I took the red paint and enlarged the lips. Then I finished with a semi-circle in the corner of the mouth.

Mother said, "You didn't leave room for the ear."

I replied, "He doesn't need ears. He has a big smile."

We decided he didn't need a beard either.

We propped up our statue with sticks. As we watched it from the street mother frowned. I said, "He looks very happy. Everyone will like him."

Coming home from school I stopped in front of the fence and looked at our art, the happy statue among flowers. It wasn't as shiny as the neighbor's and our dwarf's jacket didn't have a pocket, but it was our work and I liked it.

A week later his nose had a crack. Then his belly.

One day I came home and our statue was gone. Mother said his nose fell off and his neck had a long crack too. She put it in the trash before his head fell off. I asked why she had white gypsum powder on her arms.

"I had to break it to pieces with a hammer, it didn't fit in the trashcan. It was a real struggle to break it apart," she said.

Over time:

The dwarf was the only art mother and I created together.

Whenever I see a statue of a human being, the first thing I notice is the mouth. I'm always in awe that a tiny carving in the corner of the lips brings the statue to life and determines the expression on the face.

Radio: *Josip Broz Tito received a festive welcome in Ghana where he met with president Kwame Nkrumah, the winner of Lenin Peace prize and one of the five founders of non-aligned nations. After discussing economic relationships between our countries, they prepared initiatives for the next summit of non-aligned nations focusing on ' Recognition of the equality of all races and of the equality of all nations, large and small.' To conclude the visit, Josip Broz Tito and Jovanka Broz were invited on a safari. Reports the Tanjug news agency.*

Child: What is a safari?
Mother: Something for aristocrats. Father knows more, ask him.

CAT PARTY

I felt so guilty I couldn't even cry.

The wire mesh was stinging my fingers but father's cutting glance hurt more. He hadn't said a word since I came out, just pointed at the mesh and told me to hold it. Mother ordered me to help him.

Yesterday my sister and I built a sand castle with tall towers. I couldn't make it in a way I imagined, the towers collapsed. I went to check the drawing in my storybook then I began to read. Mother asked me if I put the bricks back to hold down the tarp and I promised I would do it later. I read another story and forgot about the bricks.

This morning father returned from a trip and discovered that the neighborhood cats used his sand for a bathroom. He was furious because on the weekend he planned to build a drainage ditch for the gutter so the rain wouldn't flow next to the foundation. He stormed to the shed and began making a wooden frame with a wire mesh.

Father's anger scared me. It was rare that I saw him furious but when it happened before, after some factory meetings, he would rush to the shed to straighten out crooked pipes. Mother told us not to follow him until he blew off some steam. When I heard the loud hammering, I imagined that he was a raging giant smashing everything to pieces. When he returned to the house his face and shirt were dripping with sweat.

My arms hurt from pressing the mesh down while he hammered the nails. I felt heaviness in my chest. It was my fault he got mad.

In the corner of the shed there was a stack of steel pipes and iron rods. Some were straight, others bent. Father had picked them up from demolished old buildings where new high-rises would be built. He planned to use these for a metal support for the new fence once he had enough money to build it.

With each blow of the hammer his face softened. I secretly wiped off a speck of blood from my thumb. He gave me a rag. "Grab with this and hold it tighter."

After he hammered in the last nail he inspected the

wooden frame. "Good," he said. I felt a little bit better too.

When we looked up a rusty color cat was digging in the sand. "Sicc, get out!" shouted father, chasing him out of the yard. "I turn my back for a minute and that sassy cat tries to piss in my sand."

It was funny but I didn't laugh. I was happy he talked because I knew he wasn't terribly mad anymore.

Cats wandered into our neighborhood. They liked the gardens. People always said "The city should do something about all the cats," but nothing happened.

People adopted some of them. When our Cirmos disappeared, father was so sorry, he didn't want to get another cat.

I shoveled the lumpy sand into the large sieve father was holding. He shook the sand out then dumped the cat poop in a bucket. There were lots of stinky lumps. Now I understood why it was important to put the bricks on the tarp. I thought it was only to protect it from the rain.

Lots of roots remained in the sieve. "Grape roots?" Father frowned. "It's probably from the Seven Oaks sand dunes." The outskirts of the town had large vineyards which meant to 'hold down' the sand when the wind blew.

My shoulders hurt from lifting up the shovel but I kept quiet. Around my feet I felt the cold air rising from the basement window. I shivered.

"What did you learn in school?" he asked.

"About the rivers in Yugoslavia. Duna, Tisza, Neretva, Drava, Sava, Vardar and others." I said in one breath.

"That's good."

"We learned how water rises to the clouds and back to

the ground," I added.

Father paused. "The Neretva river has a big hydraulic power plant. One day we'll take a trip and you can see how they use water to get electricity."

He often talked about the interesting things he saw on his trips. I imagined the places but wished that I could see them for real.

"We learned how the partisans liberated us. Then Tito and the communist party built the new Yugoslavia," I said.

He pulled out an arm-long root from the sand. I dumped three more shovels on the sieve before he spoke. "So that's what they teach you."

I stared. "That's the truth. Right?" Father was seventeen at the end of WWII when the final fighting took place. He wasn't in the army but his three brothers were. He told us many stories from that time. Then there were things better 'not to talk about.' I couldn't imagine what that would be.

He shrugged.

I said, "We had enemies who wanted to have a kingdom. The people's liberation army killed all the traitors. It says so in my book."

Father dumped the sandy cat poop in the second bucket. "War is an ugly thing." His voice was hoarse.

I nudged him to tell me more but he kept working silently. I felt bad again. I trusted my textbooks, but now I wasn't so sure.

He said, "You learn what they teach you. There are a lot of good things you can learn in school. This history is only a small part of everything. In the end it doesn't matter what they say about it."

Mother came out to check on us. "My God. This is where the cat party was. Must be breeding season."

Father grinned. "Do you want the fertilizer?"

She scoffed. "I clean that from the garden all the time. It burns the roots of my flowers." She grabbed an empty bucket. "Let's move the sand into the basement."

Father showed the sieve to her. "This would be good when I build the fence." Picking out the roots he said, "*Ajajaj*, they reassured me this was fine river sand, from Tisza. Those gangsters, they got it from the dunes when NaftaGas built the road."

Mother was leaving with a bucket full of sand. "Hurry up, it shouldn't take hours to finish up."

I still wondered about the partisans. If they did bad things and Tito was their chief, then he did unspeakable things, too. I thought he was a great leader because they taught us in school, it said so in my books. Whenever Tito travelled people greeted him with flowers. How could he be bad?

"Was Tito a bad leader?" I asked.

Father shrugged. "They say a lot of things. He is a shrewd politician and they all have enemies. Politics is a dirty thing; better not get mixed up in it."

It was hard to believe that Tito wasn't a great person. "Do you like him?"

Father frowned. "Don't politicize, shovel that sand."

We worked faster. Then he opened the basement window and dumped a shovel of sand down. Mother shrieked from below, "Are you out of your mind? I'm standing right here!"

He laughed. "I got stiff from squatting. I can just shovel

it down." He continued and mother yelled again.

"Wait until I come up. I'm going to dump the cat poop on your head."

Father chuckled. He bent down and poked his head through the window, "Plenty of space there."

"Are we done?" I asked. Half of the sand wasn't sifted.

He shoveled with great vigor. "I can clean it out later. Go and play now."

I wanted to ask mother if she liked Tito. I was looking for her when auntie Mancika walked into our yard through the little gate. Around the house we had a wire fence with metal decorations and in the back we had a 'good neighbor gate,' without a key.

Anyone could see into your yard so people were always properly dressed when they stepped out from the house. You didn't want to scandalize your neighbors.

When mother came up from the basement, auntie Mancika was holding her forehead. "My Rozsika, do you have some strong pills for a headache? I barely slept last night. Fancy that, a gang of cats got into our attic. I was sure the ceiling would collapse on our heads."

She didn't wear an apron like she always did and the edge of her lace nightgown was visible under her housedress.

Mother made a sympathetic face. Auntie Mancika continued. "I thought my head would explode last night. In the hawthorn trees in front of the house they were chasing each other. Not two or three, but it had to be a dozen cats. Then I heard them scratching the roof of Lona's shed."

Auntie Mancika sighed, "Jozsi didn't hear a thing. How

could he sleep through such a ruckus? I don't know if I believe him. Now he is in the attic looking for a hole."

I didn't hear anything either. I close my eyes in the evening and when I open them up, it's morning. Sleeping is easy. I didn't understand why many adults couldn't do it.

Mother slapped her hands. "Not enough to have a cat concert," auntie Mancika went on. "Then Bodri was barking and rattling his chain, sprinting in circles. He made a ditch where he ran."

The neighbor's bulldog was unstoppable once he began barking. He had a nervous condition. That's why auntie Lona put the doghouse as far as possible from her door, which was right next to our entrance.

Auntie Mancika nodded. "I tried to calm Bodri down, I was afraid he would choke himself with his chain. But he didn't hear me because I couldn't shout loud enough."

Mother added, "I tell you that dog is going to have a heart attack one day."

"I came out looking for Cincike," said auntie Mancika. "She is a silly young cat, I was afraid these tom-cats would hurt her. It was a full moon but I still couldn't see her."

They also had two boy cats. Did they play in our sand?

Next door, carrying a plate of leftovers auntie Lona staggered towards Bodri. She was in a nightgown, her gray hair uncombed. I never saw her without a hairdo. She dumped the scraps in a dog dish, waved to us and wobbled back inside. Bodri sat there, staring at the food.

Mother lowered her voice. "Last Monday evening a car stopped in front of Lona's house, and she saw that somebody tossed a sack on the road. Then they let the cats out." I couldn't imagine how that happened because the claws would get stuck in the woven sack. He would have to shake them out or untangle the claws. "The same car came back on Tuesday. They bring the stray cats here from the high-rises."

The neighbor whispered. "They praise the new houses, but people say it's hot in the summer and freezing cold in winter."

"Those government flats are tiny sleeping boxes where people live on top of each other. The cement blocks are this thin." Mother held up two fingers. "The entire wall is one piece, with holes for windows; it's a miracle the skyscrapers don't collapse."

"Aha, someone miscalculated the cement." Auntie Mancika circled her wrist then tapped her pocket to imply they stole it.

"My Bela saw in Bosnia that they dug out half of the mountain to make cement," said mother. "Building materials are everywhere, so they could pour thicker walls. We have riches, but the big-shots don't know how to build."

"They are in a hurry to have houses for everyone," said the neighbor.

Mother waved the air. "But what kind? There is no craftsmanship when they build with cranes. It's not a home when you don't have ground under your feet. My Mancika, I ask you, how could people keep cats when they don't even have enough space for a family?"

Auntie Mancika was leaving. "Poor animals. But I hope the cat party is over."

I went closer to the fence to watch uncle Jozsi climbing

down from the attic. The tall ladder looked scary but I would be brave enough to climb up. I wanted to see where the ball was last night. I stood there hoping he would invite me over, but he didn't notice me.

Father was washing his hands at the outside faucet when mother sprayed him with water and said, "I have sand in my hair, you hot-headed man." She tickled and pinched him. "I got you now." The more serious she got the more father laughed. He ran away, mother chased him shouting. "I'll get you."

I stared at the attic imagining what kind of footprints could be in the dust when suddenly, behind the shrubs, auntie Mancika raised her voice. "What do you mean no holes? Of course I heard them. Really, I'm getting a headache from you. Cats can't open a door."

Then I heard laughter from our house. My little sister shouted, "Wrestling!"

Then mother's laughing voice called out, "Children help me, let's knock down father." Her words were serious but her voice chimed with laughter. Any time I heard that, I forgot everything and ran towards it. I had to decide whose side I was going to be on.

Over Time:

Throughout the years my enthusiasm for Tito wavered as I heard hushed comments from adults. Father told me to stop searching for the truth and rather decide it for myself. What mattered was *who Tito was to me.*

Radio: *A two day Folk Festival is held in the Ivo Andric hall in Jajce where dance groups from all six republics compete for the titles of 'Best Ensemble, Best Solo Dancer, Best Music Group and Best Choir.'*

In the opening ceremony the festival participants laid flowers both on the 'Victims of Fascism' and the 'Bosnian grenade battalion' memorials and performed songs and recitals commemorating the sacrifices of our partisan liberation army. Tonight at 19:00 the choirs will sing on the outdoor stage by the old castle walls.

Dear listeners, we continue our program with Inspector Maigret and the Bum, by George Simeon. A radio play, part six.

WHAT IS TALENT?

In 2nd grade the whole class sang together. The *Knowledge of Society* textbook had songs for children, pioneers, and scouts. I liked the drawings of the flags, campfires and hikers. The Hungarian folk songs were decorated with tulips and roses. The pages looked like the embroidered tablecloths people get at weddings.

When I sang it felt like my body got lighter and could float. I could see far away when I followed my voice.

One day in 3rd grade I had to stand up and sing alone.

I let my voice out and I felt the breeze on my face, saw the flames, and the bells. I was happily chiming, "Bim-Bam, Bim-Bam," louder and louder feeling both the echo rushing through me and the tingling of my toes.

Teacher Bozanich waved her hand and said with annoyance, "You can't sing." She wrote a note in the grade book before I finished the song.

As I sat down I still felt the sparks of the fire popping inside my stomach. I knew all the words by heart. Why would she say I can't sing?

I listened to the others taking their turns. How come the teacher told them they could sing? I couldn't tell what they did differently.

When Marti was singing the teacher clasped her hands and beamed. "You have a beautiful voice. You're very talented! I'll talk to professor Denes. He would want you in the choir."

Marti smiled. "I sing a lot. I like it."

I raised my hand. "What does it mean to be talented and how do you learn it?"

The teacher explained. "Some people are born with talent. Artists have a special talent to sing, to paint, to be actors or sculptors."

I thought school was a place to learn everything. This was the first time I was told that you have to be born with extra stuff to do things well.

I asked her, "Do you need talent to dance? Everyone dances *csardas* and *kolo*."

"It's different because folk dance is part of life. You learn the steps, then you can do it. It comes naturally, like riding a bicycle," she said.

I understood that. Last summer I was learning to ride father's new bicycle and I almost fell off. After I drove over his foot several times he brought home a medium size bike where my feet reached the pedals. I didn't mind that it was rusty, and I quickly learned how to ride it.

"Do you have to have talent to be a ballerina?" I asked.

"Of course, they're artists," said the teacher. "Ballerinas practice very hard but if they don't have talent they don't add art to the dance."

I never thought about 'talent' and 'art' when I watched ballet on TV. I enjoyed the performances except the ending when my favorite person died. Recently I saw Swan Lake from Leningrad and Firebird on the Kiev Ballet stage. Afterwards they showed the young Russian girls in training. I felt sorry for them because they had no free time to spend with friends.

I didn't want to be an artist. I just wanted to sing well.

At the end of the class we all sang together '*Boldog kis pionir*', the Happy Little Pioneer. I felt in my fingertips the silky red flag which flew over the blue sky.

I told mother what happened in school. She smiled but her lips curled down and her eyes were shiny. "Yes, you can't sing. It takes talent. Your father can't carry a tune, I don't sing, so you couldn't inherit anything from us."

It was not often she agreed with my teacher. I felt she was mistaken too. I wasn't born with any teeth, yet they grew later. Twice. Maybe talent is like teeth, hidden somewhere and mother doesn't know about it.

She was still curling her lips. "My stepfather and his lot could sing. They were a rollicking bunch. He drank then danced on the table. I was a goose-herder at your age. He took my money ... "

Mother looked at me, "It's fine if you don't sing. There is more to life than drinking, high jinks and throwing money to the gypsy violinist."

I heard this before. Mother had cruel stepbrothers. She never talked about how they tortured her, just waved her hand and said, "It's in the past. Leave it there."

I was thinking about my hair, nails, and growing feet. With my tongue I felt a new molar breaking through my gum. "When I'm 18 I'll get four wisdom teeth. Why couldn't talent grow in me?"

Mother sighed and rubbed her eyes as she went into the kitchen. "Your father doesn't have a hearing either. You can do something else."

I didn't understand why I was missing hearing too.

I opened my textbook and sang about the mountains and freedom. Then repeated it. After that I tried a folk song about the rose garden. I knew it takes practice to learn anything well. I heard the wind blowing outside. There was nothing wrong with my ears.

In school when I sang "*Sej-haj rozsa kert*" the teacher hummed along and I was happy that she liked my singing. When I finished she frowned and wrote a number in the grade book. Edit from the front row signaled me with three fingers.

No matter how much I practiced singing, I never got a better grade than 3.

The TV aired folklore programs all the time. My favorite was the Hungarian National Ensemble from Budapest. I watched the dancing feet, the elegant shoulders, the strong fists, and the sparkling eyes. When they were all singing, "Sej-haj, sej-haj," I felt tiny bubbles tingling in my arms and legs.

In school I continued to raise my hand because I liked how singing made me feel. When the teacher said, "You don't have hearing." I asked what that means. "Somebody doesn't have a hearing when they can't tell the difference between the notes." She explained.

When I asked my friends, they shrugged.

"Just sing," said Vali.

Magdi laughed, "I can't tell the difference between notes either and my father teaches in the music school. Keep singing!"

Months later teacher Bozanich asked, "Who wants to sing *Sej-haj rozsa kert?*" I didn't raise my hand. Later she called my name because she had to give grades to everyone.

At home I had a swing next to the flower garden. I enjoyed singing as I kicked my feet and flew above the fence. My voice would travel inside me to faraway places.

I sang when the lilac bloomed, I hummed when the rose buds opened and I sang at dusk after mother watered the jasmine and before the mosquitoes arrived.

I still didn't understand what talent was or what it meant to have a hearing but I knew that singing made me feel good and I could hear the trembling in my chest.

Over Time:

Marti became a dentist but her passion for music, singing

and dancing is still part of her life. She sang in the Pro Musica Chamber Choir which performed at various festivals and concerts.

I always enjoyed singing along with others in weddings, folk-dance groups or when we danced to rock-and-roll music.

Radio: *The Pro Musica Chamber Choir will accept non-music school members into their ranks. Anyone with singing talent is invited to audition on Mondays at 18:00, Strosmayerova street 5b.*

NIKOLA TESLA STREET

For two years my friends and I never had an argument. We laughed a lot, and it was never boring to talk with them.

We lived in the section of the town called *Kertvaros*, the Garden City. Deciduous trees lined the rows of new yellow brick houses and old bourgeois buildings. Flowerbeds bloomed behind the iron fences.

When I started school only Adolph Singer street was paved in our neighborhood. Not many cars drove by except the trash trucks. Bicyclists navigated the potholes. Horse-carts trotted by with melons for sale, or with gypsies shouting that they would buy old metal.

To get to school I walked on Nikola Tesla street for ten minutes, then turned right into Baninska.

Coming home took me half an hour. Marti, Magdi, Edit, Vali and I always walked together and talked. We each had a father working and a mother at home. We all had one sibling, except Marti, who was an only child. The major meal of the day, the midday dinner, waited for us and we parted when one of us said, "I'm hungry."

We stopped on the street corner before someone had to turn from Tesla street into their street and discussed TV programs, weekend visits, ribbons and socks, and hundreds of other things.

In 3rd grade they all began to attend music school. I told my mother, "I'd like to go to music school too."

She replied, "The teacher said you can't sing. So you don't need music school."

"I want to go. They're all going," I said.

Mother lowered her head. "You don't have hearing."

"They teach ballet too, I'd like to learn it. That's the only place in town." I insisted.

She sighed. "You would have to choose an instrument and sing in a choir, too. Ballet is only one class."

I agreed to do it. She said, "I don't have room for a piano."

"I could play a flute," I suggested. "Marti, Magdi, Vali and Edit already started. Why can't I go?"

"Don't compare us to them, they're the intelligentsia. Their fathers bring home more money. Vali's and Marti's mothers are seamstresses and earn good money on the side. Your father is only a chauffeur."

"I want to learn music." I was pleading with her now.

She said, "No. We can't afford private lessons and an instrument rental. We belong to the working class. Be content to attend regular school."

I bowed my head. I didn't understand why it was expensive to learn music. The flute was a folk instrument.

It was in my storybook; the little swineherd played his flute in the barn. There were violins and accordions in folk stories, too.

Mother asked, "Do you want to go to Partizan for gymnastic lessons? It's a club membership, only a small fee."

I shrugged and went to play outside. I sat on the swing, thinking. *How come they told us in school we can learn anything we want?* Tito promised education to the working class. Now I find out there is a second school to learn music, but I can't go there.

After kicking my feet and swinging I felt better. The swing was one of my favorite things and it always helped me when I was confused.

From there on walking home from school felt different. My friends talked about music lessons and used words I didn't understand, like *solfeggio* and *alto*.

Edit gasped, "I had to play andante instead of allegro. My fingers are stiff." They learned new things and I didn't. They talked about how much music homework they have.

I said, "I had to swing on the uneven bars. My hands are dry now because I dipped my sweaty palms into chalk powder."

Marti turned to me, "You're lucky, you're free after gymnastics class. I have to do homework."

Magdi added, "Music school is so much harder."

That's when the disagreements began.

"Gymnastics is more difficult than singing. You have to use all of your muscles not just your voice," I said. "It's also more dangerous, you can fall. Did you ever see a pianist fall off the chair?"

"I must do this before each piano practice." Marti showed finger and wrist movements.

"Do you know they move the vault-board 75cm from the vault? After I jump I have to land on my feet. That's hard!" I said.

"I played the same line of music TEN times before the teacher said move on to the next one. And I have to practice it 30 times before the next class," said Magdi, holding her forehead in exasperation. "I have no free time at all."

As we walked on the sidewalk the conversation grew louder and louder. Wind blew the yellow hawthorn leaves. I was sweaty and forgot to put on my fall jacket. My throat hurt by the time I turned into our street.

Mother checked my forehead and made me a cup of linden tea. It was slimy but the honey made it better. She said, "If your throat hurts tomorrow I'll make you a steam-bath."

I hated when she put a towel over my head and a steaming bowl of salt water under my nose. I had to inhale the hot air until I got better. I usually got worse from the heat. When that didn't cure me she boiled onion skins and I had to drink that brown liquid. After a sip I wanted to throw up. I wished to get better so I could avoid the cures.

My throat recovered from the linden tea and the next few days we didn't walk home together.

Soon I learned gymnastic routines on each piece of equipment. I was excited to tell them. "The floor exercise has music. I did two gypsy-wheels, to music."

Edit said, "I broke a finger nail when playing the scale I practiced so much."

131

Magdi laughed, "The teacher said I have to play five lines of music by heart. I always looked at the notes, so I tied a shawl over my eyes."

Marti added, "I used mother's scarf. Mine was too short and I could peek out."

Vali rolled her eyes. "I hid my music upstairs and I played the piano downstairs. But I still can't play five lines."

"I had to walk on the high beams three times and spin twice. And I didn't fall down." I bragged. My voice became so loud that all the music students crossed to the other side of the street. We were shouting until one-by-one they turned right and I walked alone.

At times Vali was on my side and she would whisper to me, "Solfeggio is singing so-fa-la notes." But most often she joined the music group. Vali started gymnastics, twice a week but sometimes she had to practice the piano instead. After a while she didn't come to Partizan any more.

One day the shouting was so loud that I had tears in my eyes. That day Vali walked by my side. She was getting bored with the piano but she didn't say anything.

The others declared, "Gymnastics is not important. Nobody does it in life. Look at the musicians, they're on stage, theater, everywhere. Gymnasts are only in the club Partizan."

I defended my sport. "What about Olga Korbut? You saw her on TV getting gold medals and she'll go to the Olympics in Munchen. The competitions are in different countries and she will travel."

Magdi grinned. "She tripped on the floor exercise."

Marti said, "That's just a contest. Music is part of your life."

"When you do gymnastics the body learns to be flexible and that's part of life too. Gymnasts have good figures and strong bodies. It's important." I felt my checks flushing hot.

A woman walked by, her eyebrows pulled up. "Children, don't you know how to be nice to each other? Is this what you learned in school? Be ashamed of yourselves. What kind of pioneers are you?" She walked away shaking her head, talking to herself. "Ajjajj, all the talk of pioneers building our future. They fill their heads with ideas but don't teach them how to get along."

She spoke Serbian, but we understood it. We all stared after her.

I was never before scolded by a stranger.

I wished that we were all on the same side of the street, the way it was before music school started. I smelled the muddy road and I missed my friends very much. Nobody said anything. I went home, my cheeks flushed, my voice hoarse.

Mother gave me the onion tea. I cried. She thought I hated the tea and didn't make me finish it.

From that day on we walked on the same side of the street and we didn't mention music or gymnastics. We talked about books and the new homework. We were quiet and careful. We didn't try to outbid each other. It was good to be together.

A week later I asked Marti. "Did you learn to play the Rose Garden song?"

She replied, "On piano you play classical music. But we

started with nursery rhymes. I know *Boci-boci tarka*."

I exclaimed, "Aaaah, that's why there are no pianos at weddings when everyone sings folk songs."

Magdi said, "I'll never learn to play violin as well as the gypsies. You can't even see their fingers moving on the strings." Then she asked, "Do you see the boys doing gymnastics?"

"Sometimes, when they practice on the rings. They're usually done when we start," I said.

Marti asked, "Did you swing on the rings? You could fly very high on them."

I hadn't even thought about using the boy's equipment. On the next practice I asked the trainer and he lowered the rings for us. We had 10 minutes of free form swinging. I felt like I was flying over treetops and wished we could do this all afternoon.

One day walking home Marti said, "My mother got me a music book of popular hits. After I practiced the scales I could play whatever I want."

My eyes widened. "Does it have the Kos Janos hit? Can you play it?"

She smiled. "It takes time to learn it."

"Can I come and listen to you?" I was ready to sit by her piano.

"In a month or two," she said. I was surprised that it takes that long to learn one song. Everyone wanted to hear the famous song *'Kislany a zongoranal'*, Little Girl At The Piano. Marti promised she would ask her mother and invite everyone.

When I said "Szia" to them I felt a tingling inside me. I was glad we could talk about everything even if we didn't do everything together. As I was strolling on the last block I thought that friendship is like walking on Nikola Tesla street. We walk together from school then at each corner one of us turns into a side street to get home. Tomorrow we'll have something new to talk about.

Years later Tesla street got paved, and every half hour a Fiat would race by. We walked home together until the end of 8th grade.

Over Time:

We're still friends.

I later found out:

- Vali hated the piano lessons. She attended classes because her mother wanted her to do it. At the end of eighth grade she was glad the torture was over.

- Vali and I were waiting our turn on the uneven bars when one of the gymnasts fell off and broke her arm. The edge of the ragged bone wasn't visible and I was surprised how the skin held everything together. Vali was terrified by the incident and quit gymnastics.

- Edit struggled with singing and playing the piano yet she practiced.

- Regardless of the weather, Magdi's hands were always ice-cold before a performance or an exam. She wished she could attend drawing classes instead of tormenting everyone with her violin.

Marti loved music and still enjoys it. Both of her daughters became successful concert pianists.

Twenty years later mother told me one of her biggest regrets was that she didn't sign me up for music school. She was afraid to incur any extra expense at that time. She also felt guilty that she didn't treat her children equally.

My sister played violin and travelled with the Pro Musica Chamber Choir to places we couldn't afford to go.

I told her I had the love of books and the flexibility of a gymnast, and going to music school would have been too much.

Radio: *At the conclusion of the meeting he used Lenin's words: 'Give me just one generation of youth, and I'll transform the whole world.'*

Child: How could that be?
Mother: When the time comes, you'll learn it in school.

KISSES TO YOU

We opened our notebooks to show teacher Bozanich our math homework. Instead of walking around and checking it, she stood in front of the class and said, "I have a quick announcement. The Teachers Board decided that all students must use proper greetings. If not, your overall grade for behavior will go down. No more *Csokolom*. You greet your teachers with *Jo napot*, and when you part you say *Viszont latasra*. Especially when we have school inspections, you shouldn't say *Kisses to you* or any other phrases you heard at home. Only Good day and Good bye. Remember that."

She began to write on the blackboard the word Sub then stopped when we asked what was wrong with the greetings our parents use.

She said, "In socialism we're all equal. We don't serve

others, and you'll learn this later, there is no class difference. The old fashioned 'Kis ti hand' is a bourgeois phrase. In this country, we don't kiss anyone's hand. Our salutations reflect that."

We worried that we would forget. She said, "In school and at home use the same greetings so you don't get confused."

Viszont Latasra also meant *until we see each other* and we had many other words for parting. I said, "To the relatives we say God bless you."

Teacher Bozanich rolled her eyes. "Don't use anything with God, Virgin Mary, or saints. Especially not in school. Good day and good bye only, anything else is wrong."

We asked if we could say 'wishing you good morning' because the morning is not a day.

She sat down, rubbing her forehead. "Leave out the word 'wishing.' That's the sweet-talk of bourgeoisie. I suppose you could simply say "Good morning" at your first class of the day. Afterwards say Good day."

School began after seven, sometimes after eight. We wanted to know the exact hours until we could say 'good morning.' What should we do when we have afternoon classes?

She replied, "When it's dark, say Good evening."

"In summer," said Tomi, "it doesn't get dark until nine o'clock. When do we start saying good evening?"

This rule didn't matter to me, I was in bed by that time. Besides, during vacation I didn't see anybody from school.

Teacher Bozanich sighed. "After seven o'clock, I suppose. Enough of this." Then she finished the word on the blackboard 'subtraction.' We had twenty minutes until the bell.

Next day I helped mother in the flower garden. When I saw Auntie Confectionery walking to her mailbox I said loudly, "Good day." I wondered if I should say 'auntie' when suddenly mother slapped my mouth.

"The teacher said that's how we should greet people," I whimpered.

Mother's face was red as she looked at our neighbor. "I'm ashamed of her. This is not what I taught my children." She shook my shoulders. "Apologize for this. Now."

I didn't understand why I made her mad.

Auntie Confectionery shook her head. "It's all right Rozsika. They have the power to say whatever they want. They're the new ruling class."

Mother bent down to face me. "What's with you? This is how you show respect? Shame on you."

Auntie Confectionery waved her hand. "They don't care for manners. Rozsika, it's not her fault."

Mother's voice snapped. "What's next? She should call you comrade?"

I wasn't a baby anymore but I wanted to cry. My nose, lips and teeth hurt but I was mostly embarrassed that I seemed bad and my favorite neighbor saw mother slapping me. It always hurt when she spanked me, but being seen hurt twice as bad.

When we were in the kitchen, mother paced up and down. She mumbled to herself, "The communists are not going to tell me how to raise my children and what proper manners are."

Each time she was angry with me I felt like a canyon

opened up between us. Being separated from mother brought tears to my eyes. How could I be good if I didn't know what was right?

She faced me and said. "We live in this country, so we have to follow the rules. In school, you do as your teacher says. But at home, you do as I tell you."

I nodded. When she spoke I began to feel better.

"A polite greeting between adults is 'Wishing you a good day' or morning or evening. If a child says that to an adult it shows bad manners. I'm not raising you to be disrespectful. Clear? Children say *Szervusz* or *Szia* to each other. Same for adults who are friends or colleagues. Hello or Hi is proper because they're on the same level."

I understood that, I said Hi to my classmates. I told her what we discussed in school and how the teacher wasn't sure when the evening started.

Mother thought it over. "In the old days the greetings depended on the sunlight. The evening started at dusk when the chickens went to sleep. If all the animals were taken care of, the daily work was finished, then they said 'Wishing you good evening.' They lit the candles or oil lamps. We often burned tallow, a special kind of fat."

I liked how mother explained things. "What about the palaces and bourgeois homes?" I asked. "When did they say good evening?"

Mother laughed. "Maybe when the dancing began. I don't know. They called each other Your Grace, Honorable Lord, Venerable Lady, and had to bow and curtsey the right way. That was another world."

"They got up late," I said, "and didn't wish good morning to anybody." As we laughed, my lips didn't hurt anymore. Mother briefly touched my cheek. I wasn't sure if it was a caress, but I felt warm inside.

"We shouldn't say God bless you. Only good bye. Is that right?" I asked.

Mother shouted, "It's not their business to tell me how to talk in my own house." Then she shook her head. "I can imagine what people in factories have to swallow."

In spite of her rage and sadness, I didn't feel separated from my mother. I didn't cause her anger.

I noticed the neighbor pruning her shrub. I ran out and shouted, "Kisses to you, auntie Mancika," thinking that would cheer up mother. We were free to greet people the way we wanted.

Over Time:

I thought greetings were unimportant because they were dictated from above and could change with time.

But meeting, then parting, always meant something, no matter which words I used.

Radio: *We have over one million people in our country with higher than primary school education. We have over 5000 scientists and researchers. But we have to be watchful as we progress; our enemies are everywhere and want to destroy our socialist system.*

Child: Anyu, are you going to make a walnut cake next Sunday?
Mother: I don't know.
Child: Plum strudel?
Mother: Go and play with your sister.

THE BOY WHO TALKED TOO MUCH

I was eleven years old and I didn't have any secrets. With my friends we even talked about potential sins, whether we should confess being angry with our siblings or not.

When a new TV show started we discussed it in great detail. Vali, Magdi, Marti, Edit and I liked the *Barkoba* guessing game. Tomi was also walking with us on Nikola Tesla Street. He said, "I didn't see it. My father watched the news."

Vali said, "*Barkoba* is on the MTV channel." We had the *Magyar Televizio*, MTV from Hungary and the Serbian programs on the *Jugoslav Radio Televizija, JRT*. The official news came from Belgrade on JRT.

Magdi chuckled. "When father turns on the news my mother leaves to wash the dishes."

Marti rolled her eyes. "News is soooo boring. The way they talk is Chinese to me." We all agreed.

Magdi turned to Tomi. "What are you doing at your grandma's?"

He smiled. "Nothing. She feeds me until I'm stuffed up to here." He drew a line at his neck. "I play with the dog. She has a yard," he added. Tomi lived on the second floor of a four-story building near the E5 auto road. It was the opposite direction from the way we were going.

Magdi laughed. "Must be nice. When I visit my grandma she gives me fried chicken and all my favorite foods. She never makes me eat spinach, like my mother."

Tomi said, "My mom leaves me an egg sandwich in the fridge. Today I'll get peas and pork chops. I like how granny cooks the peas."

The girls had to hurry home to practice for music lessons. Tomi usually turned right but he continued with me on Nikola Tesla street.

I had gymnastics from 4:00 to 6:00 and was in no rush. I kept talking. "On TV they had to guess an object, 'Charlie Chaplain's hat'. That was the answer. They asked so many clever questions. The prize was tickets to a play called Orpheus."

We stopped on the corner of Nikola Tesla Street where I had to turn. As he leaned against a green wall, Tomi said. "I didn't tell everything about what happened last night. Mom told me not to talk about it."

My only secret I had already confessed in church. I was eager to find out other people's secrets. I put down my bag.

"I won't tell anyone, I promise. Please tell me," I begged.

He hesitated. "For sure?"

"Yes." I promised.

He ran his fingers through his short brown hair and said, "The TV news was a communist meeting from Belgrade, then dad cursed in Hungarian and Serbian and threw his pack of cigarettes at the TV." He paused and looked at me seriously.

I thought a secret would be more interesting than the TV program of a communist party talks.

"What did you do?" I asked, trying to hide my disappointment.

Tomi shrugged, "I picked up his cigarettes. The tobacco shreds were all over the rug. He was shaking his fist, yelling. Mom told me to play in my room. She was afraid the neighbors would hear him. You won't tell anyone?" He smiled but this wasn't that carefree grin he always had.

He trusted me with his secret and that felt really good.

"People get angry, that's nothing much. Nobody likes to listen to the communist speeches," I said, trying to be polite. I implied that this was not a real secret. I added, "My father says it's empty talk, they should be hoeing the fields instead of planning the five year future."

Tomi whispered. "We have a strange neighbor, he always finds something to complain about. Mom said I could say hello but I shouldn't talk to him. That's why she is sending me to granny now."

"Strange. How so?" I asked.

Tomi sighed. "There was a stray cat on the stairs and he saw me giving it milk. He chased the cat away, yelling at me that I'd let in any shabby animal, and he would have to call the health inspectors. Another time I practiced on my accordion and he banged on our door. I didn't open it. He shouted for a while then left. The next day dad took my accordion to granny's house."

"We have thick brick walls but mother still whispers to father if he jokes about the news. She says, '*Shhh*, the walls have ears,' " I whispered.

"A weird neighbor," Tomi continued. "We must be quiet but he turns up the radio. I can clearly hear him singing the Serbian kolo. Like an opera singer." Tomi wrinkled his forehead, then waved his hand and smiled again.

"How come you didn't talk about this before, to the others?" I asked.

He shrugged, "Mom said I shouldn't talk about this neighbor." Tomi picked up some hawthorn leaves. "You're slightly different."

"Different in what way?" I asked. I thought I was just like my friends and couldn't decide if this was good or not.

He shrugged. "Different."

I wished he said more about me. It was interesting that he knew things I didn't know about myself. But I was getting hungry, ready to say good-bye.

"My granny listens to the radio," Tomi said. "She doesn't watch TV."

"My mother likes Budapest, *Kossuth Radio.* The

Hungarian stations don't always come in clear," I added.

"Needs an antenna. The Hungarians will soon finish a new relay tower, then Jugoslav Radio won't interfere with it," Tomi concluded.

"How come you don't have to practice?" I asked.

He waved his hand. "The accordion is easy. You press the buttons with your fingers. I don't need to practice that much."

I was surprised that everything was easy for Tomi. Vali told me that she didn't choose the accordion because it was difficult to play, especially since one hand presses the buttons and the other plays on the keyboard. It's enough trouble to play the piano keys with both hands.

I picked up my bag. "I have to go."

"Do you want to know something else?" He was still leaning on the wall.

"Sure," I replied hoping it was not about another boring meeting.

"I was standing on the stairs with a bunch of other boys watching girls' legs. Collectively we concluded that Marti has the best looking ankles and you have the best looking knees."

I forgot that I was hungry. I grinned and felt warm inside. Now, *this* is a good secret.

"Doesn't everybody have good-looking knees?" I asked.

"Oh no! They're all different. Some girls have it cricked, some too bony. Legs are very different." His eyebrows pulled up, head tilted.

He gave me his expert opinion. I was impressed how observant Tomi was because I would not think to compare how legs looked.

We parted. Both of us were in a good mood.

Next time when I went up the stairs I noticed Tomi and Sanyi standing at the landing, politely letting everyone go by. Sanyi brushed his curly hair away from his eyes. I slowed down so the girl in front of me would leave and the boys could see my good-looking knees. They grinned as I walked by. I knew their secret and warmth was flowing from my knees towards my stomach.

That day I observed the girls' ankles and compared them to Marti's. I couldn't tell which were good looking. Maybe it's something boys can do better. I was good at knowing socks, knee-socks, and stockings. But all the legs were similar to me and I lost interest.

Our class had 24 students, 12 girls and 12 boys. The boys rarely talked to the girls except when they asked what the homework was. Outside, the boys would get real quiet if the girls came by.

Tomi had good grades, but, like most boys, he had trouble keeping quiet in class. When he whispered to Sanyi and laughed the teacher gave him another minus in her log book and added 'talks too much.' The teacher sighed. "Is your grandmother still staying with you?"

"No, I eat at her house, but sometimes I go home," replied Tomi.

I thought it must be lonely to unlock a door and find an egg sandwich in the fridge and nobody to talk to.

On the way home Tomi chatted with everyone. I asked my friends, "What's going on in the music school?"

Vali curled her straight blonde hair around her finger and sighed, "Too much practice."

Magdi frowned, "Musicians have no time for anything

else. I don't think I want to be one." She looked at Tomi and me. "You have time to talk. Must be nice."

They all hurried toward home. Marti didn't complain about the extra homework. I thought she really liked music.

Tomi said, "Sanyi and I put extra pepper on Gabi's sandwich and he didn't notice who did it."

We had a *school-kitchen* because the students from the Teacher Training College had to have a place to eat. Several boys from our class ate there. I brought my sandwich from home.

"What did you get today?" I asked.

"Bread with lard. Milk." He shrugged. "I'm just trying it out for a month."

"I wanted to try it too. But mother didn't want to pay for school meals."

He nodded. "Next month I'll bring my own. My mom makes good egg sandwiches."

Tomi smiled as he described how he played with the eggshells, making them into sailing boats while his mother mixed the yolks with mustard. Then he talked about Sanyi, the troublemaker. "He has so many ideas! He put his mom's black nylon stocking in his dad's briefcase --" He stopped and sighed. "Not important." I pleaded with him to continue but he said firmly. "I promised Sanyi I wouldn't tell."

We discussed the sports news in gymnastics and I showed him some moves from my floor exercise, standing on one leg.

He looked at the ground and said. "Sanyi's dad was furious and beat him with a belt. That's why he fidgeted so much today, but it still made me laugh."

I felt a knot in my stomach and lowered my leg. A few times mother spanked me with her hands and threatened me with the belt when father would get home. She said I was disrespectful when I told her she was doing things wrong. But father never spanked me with a belt.

"Did the stocking have a run?" I asked. "You have to lick your fingertips before you touch it otherwise the nylon gets caught in the rough skin. Then you can throw it away. If it's a small run you can get it fixed," I said.

He pondered. "Sanyi didn't say. His hands are always dirty and he probably doesn't lick them. His nails are chipped too."

"My mother used to get angry when she ruined her stockings. Do you know how expensive real nylons are? She has one pair and she wears white gloves to put them on because her hands are rough. I'm not allowed to walk by her side when she wears nylon stockings," I added.

"I don't think his dad was mad because of that. He is maybe moving out." Then he grinned. "I'll tell Sanyi. He could spit in his hands or something. He is very smart."

I thought if you're *smart* you get good grades, but Sanyi had bad grades. I also believed Tomi. How could you be smart if you don't do homework? Boys had sloppy notebooks, full of scribbles.

Tomi described the cartoon Zoli drew. The boys made up a comic book story. "Zoli can draw. He is the best."

He kept talking and I listened. I was surprised by how many things happened in my class which I didn't know. I learned about the boys' lives.

Next time I came down the stairs I saw Tomi and Sanyi

at the bottom, glancing up. I showed off my knees but also pulled down my skirt so my underwear wasn't at their eye level.

They seemed to like their new spot, because that's where they were all the time, grinning and whispering. I didn't feel good about that so I walked closer to the wall where they couldn't peak under my skirt. Sanyi looked especially vivacious.

Later that day a professor from the upper classes talked to Sanyi and Tomi. They both stared at the ground and their faces were red.

I walked up to Tomi. "What happened?" He was with Sanyi and other boys and wouldn't say anything.

That day when we said good bye to the music school students, Tomi didn't follow me on Nikola Tesla street.

"I have to go home, get ready for a weekend trip," he said. That meant he would veer right and I would go straight. He had already gone out of his way to walk this far.

"You're not going to eat at your grandma's?" I asked.

He shrugged. "Mom left me chicken *paprikas* in the fridge. I know how to warm it up on the stove."

I was impressed. My mother wouldn't let me near the stove unless she was there. I asked him what happened when the professor came over.

Tomi said, "Nothing. He asked what we were doing under the stairs."

"And?" I prodded, afraid of a horrible outcome.

"Nothing. He said you can wait with looking under girls' skirts. Play outside for now."

"No punishment?" I looked at him with astonishment.

Tomi shrugged.

I inquired, "Why didn't you talk to me in school when I asked you?"

He grinned, "I don't know." He had that smile when I knew I couldn't force out any more information. When I looked up he was already halfway down the street.

After that Tomi and Sanyi played outside but I noticed two other boys under the stairs, boys from a different class. I walked by the wall again.

One day, chairs and desks had been piled up in the empty space at the bottom of the stairs. There was no room to stand and look up.

Now I understood there was so much more happening in school I didn't know about, and if it mattered, Tomi would tell me about it when we stopped on the corner of Nikola Tesla street.

Over Time:

Throughout the years Tomi and I discussed everything. I learned from him how boys think, and he reassured me with a wave of his hand when something was not important.

This close friendship lasted until the second year of high school when he started to date Eva.

Today he has a nursery of exotic trees and shrubs.

Because of Tomi, I knew that a true friendship could exist between a man and a woman.

Radio: *Josip Broz Tito, the first Secretary General of the non-aligned nations met with Abdul Nasser of Egypt to discuss the five principles of the movement with a special emphasis on peaceful co-existence.*

The child played with her food. She lined up bites of green pepper in the middle of the plate, separating the bread bites from the pieces of sausage.

Child: Apu, what's non-aligned?
Father pointed to the bread: "There is communism in the world." He pointed to the sausage. "There is capitalism. We are in between. We don't belong to either group. That's what non-aligned means."

The child assembled a piece of sausage, pepper and bread and ate it. "When are we going to the zoo?"

BLACK AND WHITE

In third grade, teacher Bozanich asked us what kind of activities we do after school.

I proudly announced, "I go to gymnastics in the Club Partisan, twice a week. Thursdays I go to Faith Class because I'm getting ready for my first communion."

She said, "You shouldn't be so proud that you go to church." I looked into her eyes to understand what she meant. But she wore very thick glasses and I saw only a glass tunnel with a black dot at the end. She wrote a note in the register, shaking her head.

I sat down thinking, Why not? My Godmother was very happy when I told her what I learned. Why is my teacher annoyed with me?

When Marti stood up she quietly admitted, "I also attend Faith Class. Sometimes." Then added with confidence, "And music school, three times a week."

The teacher smiled forgivingly, "Probably your grandma wants you to go. What instrument do you play?"

"Piano," replied Marti.

The teacher made a note, with a smile.

My other friends, Vali, Edit, and Magdi admitted with embarrassment, "Faith Class, yes, I have a grandma too." Then cheerfully talked about the music school. The teacher asked them how much they practice, and many more questions.

I wished she had asked me about the gymnastic club. I was good on the balance beam and I could spin around without falling down.

When the teacher closed the class register, she said with tight lips, "Only villagers, farmers and old people believe in the dogmas of church. Uneducated people can be misled. We're teaching you everything you need. Don't listen to the priest, listen to your teachers."

I told my mother, "I might have to quit Faith Class because the teacher doesn't approve of it."

Mother was annoyed and waved her hands angrily. "Don't pay attention to that. She doesn't know what she is missing. Go to church but don't talk about it."

I still didn't understand the teacher's anger. I was happy to obey mother because I wanted to wear a pretty lace dress for the communion. Mother said I could choose the veil and the wreath. In the meantime, I kept wondering how that wafer would taste in my mouth and if I would be able to swallow it without chewing. The priest explained how they make it and I was curious if it was sweet like a wafer biscuit.

One day, mother was talking to the neighbor about making my new dress. "I'm worried my Singer machine is not good for lace."

The goldsmith's wife said, "Anna's communion dress is still in the closet, we don't know what to do with it. If it fits Eszter, take it."

Mother was very happy. Anna was a year older than me and had many pretty clothes. Her father worked in Aurometal, the clock-factory. They were rich because he fixed watches and made gold jewelry after work. Father said it was 'under the hat' money. The factory job was 'pro-forma' to avoid questions.

I liked Anna, and she was smart.

Mother explained to me, "You only need it for one day, it's all right to wear a hand-me-down." I knew she didn't like us to wear old clothes but she was worried about sewing a fairy tale dress for me.

When I tried on the lace dress it touched the ground. I was happy. I would look like Snow White.

Mother said, "If you want, I can cut off the bottom and

make it knee-long."

"No!" I cried out. "I want a long dress."

We had one bridal store on Rudics Street, just before the cheese market. Every two weeks they put out new wedding photos. I always stopped by the window to admire the bridal dresses, the veils and the photos. The brides looked dreamy and happy.

I was excited to get a new veil and wreath. We went to the store and I showed mother the one I liked. It was a long veil made of soft muslin. Wearing that I would be like a princess. I loved it.

Mother looked at the small tag and said, "This is for brides."

"How could they write such a long word on a tiny paper?" I asked. The Hungarian word for bride is *menyasszony*, meaning heavenly woman.

As I reached for the tag she took my hand and led me to the back of the store, "Look! These are for first confession."

They were short, touching the shoulder. I wanted a long veil to reach my feet.

She added, "A long veil would cover up your lace dress."

I had three types to choose from. They were all the stiff kind, where the veil stood away from the head. The edges had a fine finish and the veil was full of tiny embroidered flowers. I tried on all three then chose one.

When I asked my friends about their dresses, they shrugged. Vali said, "Mother will make me one."

Marti added. "Mine will sew a new dress, too."

"Is it going to be long?" I asked.

Vali shrugged. "I don't know, she won't make it until spring."

By the time I had my first communion, Anna's dress was only ankle high. That time I had a pair of white lacquered spring shoes which looked fine, except that they had a black buckle. How could I be Snow White with black buckles? I wasn't getting new shoes and had to accept the old ones.

I had a pearly white purse, white lace gloves, and I was all set for the big occasion. I liked my lace dress and all the nice things I wore that day.

My friends all had new dresses and new shoes as well. I was surprised their dresses were only knee-long. Vali said in her matter-of-fact tone, "I could wear this on Sundays."

The church was surrounded by a fence which had large iron gates. The gates were open that day and we gathered in the churchyard. There were many girls I had never seen before. Mother whispered to me, "They live in nearby villages. Many of them are daughters of rich farmers."

Everywhere I turned I saw pretty lace, embroidery, and shiny satin. One girl wore the long muslin veil I liked so much. I didn't tell her it was the wrong veil for this occasion. I didn't want to ruin her special day.

Father Wurtz had a white lacy gown over his black robe. He also prayed for us in Latin, his gray eyes half closed. I wasn't sure if this was his holy look or if he was tired.

We knelt in front of the altar to receive the sacrament. I was very careful not to bite the priest's fingers when he put the wafer on my tongue. I smelled the starch on his crisp white sleeve. I kept my mouth wide open expecting to feel sacred. I didn't taste anything, I didn't feel anything. Then I remembered Father Wurtz had told us it may take a few days before we realize how special this sacrament is. We will feel it inside.

After the ceremony we lined up in the churchyard to take photos. Magdi tucked in a lock of hair. "I slept in curlers but it's already straight. I'm not going to torture myself like my sister." She pointed at my naturally curly hair. "You are lucky."

"I like yours, it's easy to comb. My locks get tangled, then the brush gets stuck," I said.

The photographer was adjusting and arranging us for a long time. I was kneeling in the front row. I wanted to look holy on this special day so I tried to remember the sacred Latin words from the service. When somebody squinted the photographer checked everything again because you couldn't have such a special photo with your eyes closed. Then the veils covered the girls standing behind.

I noticed the women were setting up snacks on tables covered with crisply ironed white tablecloths. If teacher Bozanich would see how nicely the napkins were folded maybe she wouldn't be upset about my going to church.

Father watched me with a smile that always made me feel warm inside. My Godmother beamed at me. "Esztike, smile. Keep smiling."

I had bony knees. It was hard to kneel and smile.

"Don't fidget," said my mother.

Finally we had a good photo and I headed for the snacks.

I just started to sample a salty biscuit when a nice-smelling lady wearing a fuzzy orange suit asked me gently, "Could you pose with my son for a photo?"

She had her own small camera. Everyone in the churchyard wore nice clothes that day but she was the most elegant in her wool jacket.

I swallowed the food and followed her towards the gate. I wondered why she trembled because it wasn't cold.

Mother quickly intercepted us. "Why are you leaving?" She asked me in a stern voice, but she was looking at the lady.

I knew unless she changed her voice, I would not be allowed to go anywhere. I stopped.

"Are you a journalist, or what?" She asked the nice lady in an icy tone. Only journalists and professional photographers had their own cameras.

The lady explained in a gentle voice, "No, we're visiting from Belgrade and would like to have a special photo of this beautiful ceremony. We don't have churches like this. We don't have communions like this."

I was surprised that the capital city with one million people didn't have churches. We had 100,000 people and more than eight big churches and many small chapels. Mother glanced at the lady's husband who was pacing outside the fence, looking at the ground. She sighed and I knew I could have my photo taken for the second time. Mother walked with me then stopped near the entrance.

I stood next to a blond boy in front of the iron gate. The lady was fast with the camera, and it didn't take her long to adjust our pose.

"I'll send you a photo if you like," she said.

She wrote down our address in a hurry. Her elongated letters made the handwriting look elegant. My letters were round and fat, or too thin. I always got a minus for my handwriting.

Her pacing husband quickly took the boy's hand and hurried towards the main road.

Mother had a gentle voice when she looked at the lady, "Why don't you come inside and have some pastries?"

The lady thanked her with a smile, "We're in a hurry. I must go." She glanced towards her husband but kept smiling at the girls in the churchyard.

I was sorry that she had to rush after her husband when she really wanted to see all the girls' dresses. Why was she trembling on a sunny day?

Then I hurried back to the tables looking for strudel.

In the coming days I was waiting to feel holy but nothing happened. I couldn't ask my teacher, she would get angry again. I was a little worried that I didn't do it right. Maybe I should have swallowed the wafer faster.

Two weeks later I was surprised to receive a letter from Belgrade. The woman in the orange suit had kept her promise. And the picture was in color! I loved it. I looked a little green but this was my first color photo. I felt heavenly.

Over Time:

My bridal veil was floor length and I felt like a princess.

Radio: *This weekend Anton Chehov's Cherry Orchard will premiere in the 'Nepszinhaz.' Saturday at 19:00 is a performance by the 'People's Theater Hungarian Company. Sunday at 18:00 the 'People's Theater Serbo-Croatian Company' will perform.*

THE ONE SHOE

I dashed into the kitchen when I smelled something baking. "I want to lick the bowl." But mother had already washed everything, and it was time to slice the pastry. When she cut it into diagonal pieces there were lots of triangles and odd shapes 'not fit for serving on a platter/

"You can have the edges," she said. It was a snack, not dessert. I didn't have to eat vegetables first so the pastry tasted even more flavorful.

We were expecting father to arrive home after a four-day trip. Mother always cooked a good dinner when he returned because he didn't get proper home cooked meals on the road.

On the radio, bells tolled. It was noon. I set the table for four because father could walk in any time. The midday dinner was our major meal. We ate soup, grits-dumplings, carrots and meat patties. When the pastry crumbled in my mouth I wished father was here to enjoy the sweets too. I wondered if he was late because the director told him to drive to a castle.

When we finished eating we cleared the table but left father's plate.

It was a cold winter day but my sister and I went outside. After running we played 'statues.' First I was the sculptor. Gizi had to allow me to arrange her pose. I lifted up her left leg then bent her right arm to pull her left ear, then moved her left arm to touch her nose. I stepped back to admire my work while she wasn't allowed to move. She was a marble statue. I adjusted her shoe, it was slipping down when she couldn't hold the giggles back and lost her pose. "My turn, my turn, let me do it!" She was laughing.

Gizi made me hold my tongue, tilted my head, made me bend down and lifted my right leg up. She waited for me to tip over but I held the pose. I often played this game with my friends and no matter how much they tried to distract me I was able to stand on one leg until everyone around me got bored.

My little sister lifted my left arm to hold my right ear. She waited. I didn't move. She would have to say 'the statue is done' which meant I was the winner.

She moved my fingers to pinch my chin instead of my tongue and said, "Don't move. Let's play dishrag."

I was confident I could win both games.

"What's your favorite book?" she asked.

"Dishrag." I replied in a serious voice. If I laughed I would lose.

"What's your nicest summer dress? Tell me, tell me."

She grinned.

I swayed when I said, "Dishrag" but steadied myself. I always imagined the words and this time I had to think about my left foot instead of a stinky dishrag dress.

"What is your favorite…" she was chuckling and finally uttered, "ice cream flavor?"

"Dishrag." I burst into laughter, touching the ground. I even forgot that I had lost the game.

We headed inside asking questions, trying to look serious.

"What do you put in the cake? Fancy that, dishrag." I wiped tears from my face.

Wearing her housedress, mother hurried to the street corner several times to check if father was coming. Afterwards she had to stand by the tile stove to warm up. If I had gone outside without a coat I would have gotten into trouble.

I decided to practice reading. The Pioneer Union announced the dates for all the competitions. Last year I won a prize in the 'szep-olvasasi', nice-reading contest. My prize was the 'Book of Fairy Tales.'

I started a new story, 'The Magician's Gift' and read it out loud. I heard rummaging in the other room and was about to tell Gizi to be quiet when I remembered what the teacher told me. 'Imagine the words and see what you read. If the truck honks under your window you think it's a sound far away behind the Kingdom of Ice.'

I didn't scold my sister. As I read I pictured the flute and the fiddle. I could feel them in my fingers playing on the zither and could see the hangman dancing. At the end I felt the excitement of getting the crown and the kingdom.

When I closed the book I smelled vinegar.

My sister was under the table playing with her doll. She whispered, "Psst, Katika fell asleep. She liked the story."

All the doors were open. Mother squatted in front of the tub in the bathroom and polished the clean tiles with vinegar.

She smiled at me, "It was very nice. Would you read another one?"

After supper we were in pajamas. As the rooms aired out, Gizi snuggled in mother's lap, and I sat up straight in the armchair and read "The Castle of Crow's Rock."

Each day at 19:30 Gizi and I watched the puppet show for kids. *Raisin's Adventures* always ended with his brushing his teeth and going to bed. At the end it said 'Good Night Children' then my sister and I went to bed, too.

Next morning the neighbor, Aunt Lona shouted across the fence. "Rozsika, Bela called. He said he'll be home in the afternoon."

On our street, two houses had telephones. If it was important, father could call Aunt Lona.

Mother asked many questions. Aunt Lona lifted up her arms. "I don't know. Still in Slovenia. He is coming home."

Mother inquired. "You talked to him? What happened?"

Aunt Lona hurried inside. "I'm very cold. He is coming."

Aunt Lona wasn't as kind to me as all the other neighbors. Mother said she was a grand dame before the war. Still is. They had a factory, land, and owned this whole street when it was an empty lot. They were still very rich.

In the afternoon father walked in wearing his sweater, holding his bag.

He looked different. His face was pale as ashes. We usually ran to him, kissed him then checked his pockets for chocolate. This time we just stared.

He said, "We came home by train."

"Where is your coat?" Mother asked.

Father shrugged. "In the car." She clutched her hands.

He said, "The road was steep with patches of thin ice. I used the brakes but the wheels didn't lock. Then I pressed the clutch to downshift but it wasn't enough to stop. I couldn't steer to make the curve so we went over the cliff."

Mother held her chest and moaned. "I knew something was wrong. My sweet God, you protected our family."

"How long did you slide?" I asked.

He said, "It happened so fast, one moment I was driving, the next moment we were flying."

Mother shrieked.

"How deep was the cliff? How many times did the car roll over?" I asked.

He shook his head. "I don't know. It was a long way down. More than once. Then the car slid. We had time to say good bye to each other."

"What else did you say?" I asked.

"Nothing. We all just thought of our families." He said this in a strange voice.

I didn't know anyone who had a car accident and I never read a book about it so I didn't know what was the right thing to think about if a car was rolling down.

Father trembled when he sat down. Mother warmed up the soup.

Gizi hung upside down on the chair. "Your head was like this?"

He nodded. "Shoes and feet everywhere. Arms tangled."

"How did you get out of the car?" I asked.

He took a few spoonfuls of soup. "I can't remember. We managed somehow."

I often saw father tired and hungry after he worked around the house but he always smiled and his face shined with sweat. I never saw him this tired and his skin so gray.

He continued, "At first, Pero said we should shout for help then wait for the police to cut the door open. When I told them the gas tank was upside down and the car could explode any minute they found a way out so fast, *ahhh*. The road was high up, they climbed back up, over the rocks when I was still down. It took me a while to gather the car documents. I found my bag, too. They yelled from the road, 'Bela, leave everything.' I couldn't open the trunk to get our coats. I thought to hit it with a rock to break the lock but I was afraid to shake the car. Pero shouted, 'Bela, hurry up, it'll explode.' "

Mother held the wooden spoon in the air, the stew bubbled on the stove.

Father said, "We waited for a car to come by when Pero noticed he had only one shoe."

"Did he go back for the other shoe?" Gizi asked.

Mother laughed then wiped her tears. Father chuckled

and his ashen face got a little color. "No. There was snow and ice but we didn't feel the cold."

"How long did you wait?" I asked.

"Not long. A car came by. We asked them to call the police. Ivo, our marketing manager couldn't talk for an hour."

Mother held her throat. "Oh my God."

"How did Pero travel on a train? In one shoe?" Gizi asked.

"They gave him an old pair, they wobbled on his feet. He only took one. His leather shoe was custom made. He didn't want to leave the good one behind. They offered us shabby old coats but I didn't want one."

He waved his hand. "I had to blow in a bag, walk in straight line and answer many questions. Pero vouched for me that I never drink, but the police even took my blood. At the end they gave me a bunch of forms to fill out."

Father didn't mind getting oily or dirty but he loathed paperwork. He didn't like policemen, either.

"They gave us tea." Then he continued. "Ivo had a scratch on his chin -- cut it when he crawled through the broken windshield. They put a bandage on it. These policemen were very decent. Slovenians."

Father showed the tiny cuts on his hand. "It's from the rocks and metal when we got out."

As father spoke I imagined everything. I saw the cliff, the destroyed car, the shrubs, the rocks, the man in one shoe climbing back to the road, father prying open the trunk.

Mother asked, "How did you have money for the

train?"

Father replied, "I had the vouchers for gasoline and 60 dinars for one meal. Pero had 40 dinars. He called his wife and the factory, signed papers, and then the police gave us money. For a hotel and train."

Gizi asked, "Is the man going to wear different shoes now?"

Father chuckled. "We sat on the train for ten hours. Pero talked about how bad the factory-made shoes are. The glue doesn't hold, from the synthetic material you get calluses. He gave a speech about craftsmanship, the stitches in the leather and his favorite shoemaker who would make one new leather shoe for him. But he wasn't sure if he could order only one."

Mother patted father's face and kissed him.

He shook his head. "The policemen were amazed when they checked the identity cards. We were all born in the same year, 1928. We didn't know that before. A month ago a car went down at the same place but nobody survived. They couldn't believe we walked out from that wreck."

Mother slapped her hands. "My sweet God."

He continued. "They said probably the seat belts saved us. Uco always told everyone to buckle up. At first I didn't like the belts, but he wouldn't let me start the car until I fastened myself in. I got used to them and even when he wasn't in the car we still buckled up."

Mother said, "You're such a headstrong Hungarian. Now you owe your life to him. All of you."

"Pero will take Uco on a fishing trip to thank him," he said. I had travelled only in the Zastava 750, and there were just seats.

I asked, "What belt saved you?"

Father slurped the warm soup then said, "This belt goes over your chest, it's attached to the chassis in two places. It keeps you in your seat. The cars normally don't have seat-belts. But Uco saw a Mercedes with a German license plate and asked them what the belts were for. He spoke enough German to find out how that worked. He didn't rest until he found a way to get it installed in our Fiat 1300."

After father ate we followed him to the living room. When he came home we usually climbed on his back, or he would swing us. He was strong and it was good to play with him. This time was different.

Gizi yelled *"Birkozzunk"*, 'let's wrestle' and pushed father's arm down. He winced. She was surprised to win so fast.

Mother prepared his pajamas. "Leave Apu alone, he has to rest."

He stood up. "Let me do some work. It's time to check the apples." During winter we kept the apples in crates in the basement. If one rotted, all the others did too, so every two weeks we sorted through them.

I overheard father's voice from the basement. "I didn't want to mention it in front of the kids. Lucky thing was that Uco wasn't with us. Pero and Ivo like to sit in the back to chat. But Uco always sat in the front and that seat was smashed to smithereens. If he was in the car he would be dead now." I heard him moan then the breaking of wood.

Mother carried the crate to the living room. Father separated the good apples from the blemished ones. She told me to practice for the contest.

I read out loud the 'Talking Grape, Smiling Apple,

Tinkling Peach.' I could see the magic orchard, the carriage stuck in the mud, the pig helping the king, then taking the king's daughter in a wheelbarrow. It didn't matter that Gizi was teaching her doll somersaults, I enjoyed the story.

When I finished, father patted my hair. "You read nicely." He handed me the biggest apple from the crate.

At 19:30 the whole family watched *Raisin's Adventures.*

The piggy planted a pumpkin seed and checked it every minute to see if it was growing. We chuckled when Raisin wondered how big the pumpkin would be by the morning. Everything was more interesting when we were together.

When the screen showed 'Good Night Children' we all went to bed.

I was restless and couldn't fall asleep right away. I wondered if a squirrel could live in Pero's leather shoe, like in one of the stories I read. Then I imagined the Fiat 1300 tumbling down. I was scared and calm at the same time. Somebody protected father and his colleagues. Angels? Godmother? Fairies? God? I didn't understand but I knew they were not alone when they rolled down the cliff.

Over Time:

Ever since then I believe there is a Guardian Angel watching over me.

Radio: Classical music plays.

PRIZE

I tried to keep up with mother but she walked briskly, holding my hand. I was several steps behind her and my shoulder hurt. I said for the tenth time, "Slow down." She did but after a few steps she sped up again.

The town hall clock chimed five times.

"They just opened. We're almost there." In the afternoon the stores were open from 5:00 to 8:00. In the morning they were open from 8:00 to12:00 so factory workers from the second shift could go shopping, too.

We had two expensive bookstores, *Forum* and *Napredak* where they sold only books and maps. The other stationery stores had textbooks, paper, and everything else I needed for school.

I never bought real books before so I wasn't sure what I had to do.

But I knew how to buy textbooks. A week before school started we went to the stationery store, mother told them which grade I was in. They put together a stack of books and notebooks. Then mother paid.

That spring day I was getting my prize and we headed towards Forum. We were on the promenade Korzo when I let go of mother's hand and stopped. "You're pulling my arms out!" I yelled.

She stared at me in a strange way. "Shhhsh. Let's go." I didn't move. I was angry that she didn't listen to me.

"I won't hold your hand," she promised. Her voice was hoarse and her dark eyes shiny. I could tell she was sorry. We continued to walk and she tried to take small steps but often had to slow down so she wouldn't get ahead of me.

The *Forum* bookstore was on the promenade. The marble stairs were slippery so I held mother's hand to climb up.

The entrance had double glass doors with a wood frame. I opened the first door, wiped my shoes on the mat, then opened the second door and I smelled the fresh paper. The store was big, almost the size of my classroom. It had light brown oak shelves. In the center display the books were stacked up to form a pyramid. They were open so I could see what was on the pages. The sidewalls had floor-to-ceiling shelves with lots of books.

A man in a suit and tie greeted us. "How can I help you?"

Mother showed him my certificate which said *'Forum Nice Reading Contest. Third prize. A value of 450 dinars.'* Father's monthly salary was four times that. This competition, like many others was planned by the Pioneer Union. The contest lasted two days in Novi Sad. I slept in the Pioneer Hall because I advanced to the finals and had to compete twice.

The man smiled, "Congratulations. You can choose anything you want. From all the shelves." He pointed to the side shelves and looked at mother. "Novels too."

Mother shook her head, "No, no, it's only for her. She won it."

I never shopped for real books and I didn't know where to start. I picked up the first one I could reach on the lower shelves. It had nice pictures but not much to read.

Mother said, "You could buy it but that has only one story. This one has many more fairy tales."

I wasn't sure if I was supposed to just point to a book and say this is what I want. I began to read it from the first page but wasn't sure how much I was allowed to read.

I saw maps on the wall: the whole world, or just a continent. My school had large maps like these.

I found the new issue of the Marika series, this one 'Marika Rides Her Bike.' All of my friends had a few books from the series of Marika's adventures. When it was time for gifts, girls always asked for it.

Mother smiled as she took books from the upper shelves. "Look, you could have this one or this one." I couldn't hold them anymore. I was a little confused because I didn't know how to choose a book but I knew mother would help me. This was a fancy bookstore and everything was good here.

Each time I chose one, mother showed me another. "Or you could have this one." I glanced at the pictures but it was hard to decide because I couldn't read the whole book.

I looked at my mother and liked how happy she was. She giggled and laughed as she leafed through the pages. She bent down to show me the nice drawings, our heads touching, and we both took a deep breath.

"They smell new," she whispered to me. "They're so pretty -- and you can have them!"

I often went to the library. I held books that had water stains, torn pages, and smelled like mold, grease or dirt. Sometimes mother aired out the room if I read a very old book.

I clutched the first book I found while mother unloaded the upper shelves. My arms were full when the man in a suit made room on one of the tables. Mother laid down all the books and calculated how many we could buy. I didn't realize I could have so many. I had a few new books from previous contests but this time I was getting my own library.

I liked the titles: 77 Folk Tales, collected by Benedek Elek, Hungarian Tales collected by Gardonyi Geza, Cickafark by Mora Ferenc, Fairyland's Gate, 365 Stories, a Story For Each Day, The Prince and the Beggar.

Mother sighed. "Too much. I have to put back something." She pursed her lips, unable to decide which one. "Do you really want this?" She held up 'Marika's Adventures.'

That was the only one I knew I really liked. I said, "That's the most popular series for girls. The pictures are beautiful. Look, she rides a bike with the cat in the basket."

Mother opened the cover. "Gilbert Delahaye, Marcel Marlier, French translation. Of course. This cost more than the *77 Hungarian Fairy Tales*. This is for little kids, all pictures. You're in third grade."

"I like it. You don't know how hard it is to find them in the library. In one of them somebody cut out her apron."

This was the latest in the series, fifteen more

adventures were in the store but I didn't dare to choose more than one.

Mother put Marika next to the book of Hungarian fairy tales. "20 pages, 500 pages. They cost the same. Do you think this one is worth it?"

I sighed, and returned Marika to the display.

Mother said, "We are still over the prize money."

At the end she paid extra and I got eight storybooks. We bought almost all the ones from the top two shelves.

They wrapped the books in brown paper. I wanted to carry all of them but mother wouldn't let me. I carried a small bundle. It was heavy but made me feel grown up.

Mother was more excited about my prize than I was. As she walked slowly next to me, she talked. "When I went to school I had a black slate, this small, we called it a *pala tabla,* a blackboard and wrote on it with a chalk. We didn't have books, especially after the war." She stroked my hair then asked, "Do you want to keep them in the cabinet next to the glass vase? I'll make room." I agreed. I wanted to make sure the books stayed nice and clean.

My other books came from teachers and relatives. They handed me one and I thanked them. Buying real books was harder then buying textbooks because I had to choose. I was a bit sad that I couldn't buy the whole Marika series.

Then I felt the weight of my bundle and I was happy about my little library. I could read for a long time.

Over Time:

Over the years the white pages turned brownish but these books never got that old book smell.

They are a classic collection, entertaining even today and worthy to travel with me across the ocean to the United States. I read them to my son and still keep them on my bookshelf.

Radio: *For the month of August the Sever factory shuts down for the annual vacation. 3% of the employees will remain to oversee the maintenance of machines and assembly lines.*

Workers who plan to spend two weeks with their families in the company resort on the Adriatic Sea or in the Slovenian Alps could choose between two shifts. From August 1st through the 15th or the second shift from the 15th through the 31st. The transfer by buses is included in the price. The company reported that the workers' contribution for lodging, meals and transportation is priced to be affordable for everyone.

Last year's complaints about the lack of mosquito nets have been resolved. In all bedrooms one window has a mosquito net. They asked the people not to bring fly-swatters and not to smash the insects on the freshly painted walls.

THE CHERRY RED BIKINI

Mother made all our clothes except coats, socks and underwear. She bought clothes for father because she didn't know how to sew men's shirts or pants.

We had an old Singer sewing machine which father got from a purse maker. When he brought it home it was broken. Father fixed the machine and got a table for it.

Mother didn't have to use the neighbor's machine any more. She didn't like complicated patterns or collars. Sleeves were complicated. She would take apart old pajamas, pin the sleeve to a new fabric and draw lines around it with chalk. She would measure me then make the sleeves longer or wider.

If I got a new dress my little sister would also get a new dress. Mother said "When I was little I always had to wear hand-me-downs. I treat you equally, so you'll both get new outfits." That didn't apply to everything. My sister inherited my coats and shorts as I outgrew them.

The swimwear usually lasted two summers. My little sister and I had only the bottom part of a bikini which was low cut and ruffled.

I was ten years old when I told mother "When you make my bikini for the summer I need a top too." She looked at me and said, "You don't need one."

"I can't sleep on my stomach any more, there is a lump under my nipples." I pulled up my shirt to show her my chest. She looked and looked. "I don't see anything," she replied.

I knew sewing a bikini was complicated and expected she would say 'no.'

I turned to the side and pressed on my nipple. "You see, it goes in, then pops out. That's my breast. I can't go to the beach without the top part of a bikini."

Her lips were twitching when she bent down to pick up a crumb from the rug. "All right, I'll make you a top for your bikini."

The tiny lump under my nipple was very soft. I turned

to mother. "I'm afraid it will burst if I sleep on my stomach or push it harder."

Mother laughed then turned serious. "Don't worry, it's strong. It's natural because you're growing. And stop pushing it!"

"I didn't wash my chest for five days because it hurts when I rub it with a towel. Are you sure it's not going to burst?" I asked.

She was serious. "I'm sure." She lifted her apron and dabbed my arm. "This is how you dry your chest. But rub the towel on the rest of your body harder."

If mother wasn't worried then I knew I was all right. I resumed washing my chest.

Mother waited until late spring to prepare our summer clothes. We tried on each outfit and she checked what could be let out or lengthened and what should be replaced.

She showed me three pieces of fabric and I chose cherry red cotton for my bikini. For the bottom she sewed a ruffle on the front part, put elastic in the waist and tights to keep the bikini snug. Although the fabric was stiff mother made it fit perfectly.

For the top part she cut a wide ribbon, stitched a decorative white zigzag ribbon on it, then put elastic in it all around. She added shoulder straps so it wouldn't fall down.

When I tried it on I liked my grown up look. Mother kept repeating, "You don't need to wear it, nothing shows."

I asked her, "Can you make it wider to cover more of my chest? Like the picture in the newspaper."

She shook her head. "This is good so your skin will get lots of sunshine. It helps you grow."

I thought that next summer I would need a new bikini top again.

"At least at home don't wear it so your body gets enough sunlight," said mother.

"But the neighbors will see me," I replied.

When my sister saw my bikini she demanded a top part also. Mother sighed and cut a pink ribbon to match the pink bikini bottom. She didn't even argue with a skinny six-year-old who had nothing to cover up.

That summer we went to a thermal spa in Hungary because mother needed therapy for her backaches.

I walked with confidence in my cherry red bikini. When we saw the pool, my sister and I raced to get in first. After I jumped in, the water pushed my top almost to my neck. I quickly adjusted it underwater. My sister untangled her bikini top and handed it to mother. She didn't wear it in the pool anymore.

I enjoyed my new bikini all summer even if I couldn't do everything I used to do. When I built sandcastles the sand stuck all over the cotton and scratched my chest. Showering or dipping in a pool wasn't enough. I had to take off the bikini top and hand-wash it.

At the end of the summer I often checked how dark my skin got. Before I buttoned up my blouse I compared the white stripe on my chest to the dark brown of my stomach. When I was dressed up I knew beneath I was still wearing my bikini.

In the fall I took quick baths. I rinsed my skin and lightly dried it, afraid to rub off my tan. By the end of

November my body didn't show any trace of my cherry red bikini.

Over Time:

During the summer vacations when I was in college, I looked for topless beaches to get an even tan.

Radio: *Stane Matovich, the leader of the Economic Council declared, "We have to line up to become a tourist destination of western Europe. Our land is rich in natural beauty, the Adriatic coast and the Slovenian Alps are already well known. The aim of the Communist Party is to develop a tourist industry in the mountains, by the lakeshores and rivers to bring in foreign currency.*

At the same time we want our people to enjoy what is ours. Factories will continue to build vacation complexes for their workers."

WHAT IS A GOOD GIFT?

I carried a shiny black vase in my hand. It wasn't ordinary black. Depending on the light you could see a purple or bluish-green shimmer. Mother let me choose it for a year-end gift for teacher Bozanich, who had taught us for three years.

Near the end of 4th grade she said, "Do not buy anything for me because I got so many things throughout the years that my house is full of knickknacks."

A year before I gave her a tiny porcelain pigeon. It had nice eyes but it was only decoration. My vase was useful and artistic and I knew she liked art.

Mother told me that several parents decided to buy a gift together but she didn't participate. "We can't afford an expensive gift. They carry things too far, the intelligentsia," she said and curled her lips, like she wanted to say more but didn't.

I knew from Vali that four of my friends signed the back of a large painting. She said, "The teacher told us which artwork to buy so it's not going to be a surprise."

On the last day of 4th grade we were sitting in class, the girls wearing festive summer dresses, the boys wearing shirts and ironed pants. Even the boys' hands were clean. When the teacher called my name, she read the grade card. "Overall outstanding grade, all 5's and exemplary behavior. The Teacher's Board awarded you a certificate of merit. Congratulations, Eszter."

She showed the certificate to the class. The edge of it folded in half and underneath was a drawing. When I saw the happy kids and the sun I thought about summer vacation.

The teacher said, "This artist's drawing illustrates that the little pioneers are building the future and there is no limit to what you can achieve." Then I noticed that the kids were cheering at the spaceship headed for the sun.

When I gave her my gift, she glanced at it. "Thank you. Put it on the table." I turned it around slowly so she could notice the greenish-violet shimmer on the black. The light wasn't bright enough to see it well and she had already called "Berkes Sanyi."

When Marti, Magdi, Vali, and Edit walked up to receive their grade cards they said a gift was coming later.

The teacher smiled and nodded. They also received the certificate with the spaceship.

Vali whispered to me, "It's in the hallway, guarded by the parents. They couldn't decide which side to show first."

After the last student, Szikora Zoli, got his grade card, the doors opened. Four mothers carried in the large painting, the back of the canvas facing us. They smiled and showed the signatures and poems written on the back of the frame. When they turned it over the teacher finally saw the large horse. She clapped her hands in amazement and laughed. "Ahh, how beautiful, thank you." She couldn't stop saying thank you.

Vali was mistaken, the teacher was surprised.

It was a calm horse but I didn't like the orange meadow, which looked like it was on fire. The horse wouldn't just stare at you if the grass was burning.

The mothers turned the painting over and read the messages written by my friends. My teacher really liked that horse and kept saying, "Wonderful. It'll be perfect in my living room, thank you very much."

I concluded this was a really good gift for her. I waited around hoping the teacher would let me sign the frame. When nobody gave me a pen I felt bitterness trickling down my throat. They were excited and talked about the horse for a long time. When I nudged Vali to leave she said, "We're not going home. We'll carry the painting to the teacher's house."

I walked home alone, thinking the roses hanging over the fences might scratch the painting and wondered how my friends would fit on the sidewalk holding the frame together. Then the scent of roses reminded me it was summer and the beginning of vacation. I was happy but I also liked to be in school, to learn about the world and be with my friends. The next time I walked on this street I would attend upper classes with separate teachers for each subject. I wasn't a little kid anymore.

I missed my friends, but when I wasn't talking all the time I could think better.

I gave my mother the grade card and the certificate. She kissed me and hugged me and held me in her arms saying, "Praiseworthy results. You were so diligent." She kept repeating "well done," holding me tight. I felt tingling everywhere on my body and didn't want my mother's embrace to end. She usually gave me only a quick hug or a kiss because she was afraid she would spoil me if she hugged me too often.

She said, "Keep working hard in 5th grade too, there is more to learn." I didn't hear the words very well, I enjoyed that she was kissing my head. She talked some more then went to the pantry looking for walnuts.

When father came home I ran to him with my little booklet. He laughed and kissed me. "What a smart girl you are," he said.

He put his arm on mother's shoulder so he could look at the grades too. They read it out loud. "Native language, Hungarian, 5. Serbian language, 5. Knowledge of Nature, 5. Basis of Technology, 5." They went through every line, nodding approvingly at how many things I had learned.

Father examined the booklet. "It's all handwritten with nice letters. Your teacher had to do this for all of the kids?"

Mother pointed at the last line. "See this? Exemplary

behavior. Signed by the teacher and the director of the school. Stamped."

Father rubbed his eyes and said, "Congratulations. The excellent grades are a gift to us. But the knowledge is a gift for you."

The way father smiled at me felt like he had caressed my heart.

I headed for my swing when he embraced mother. He said to her, "Tito kept his promise, he really built good schools. Now they even teach art."

Mother replied. "What about us? All the blisters I got from pushing the wheelbarrow, all the mandatory volunteer work in youth brigades. We built it too."

Father said. "That's how it was back then."

On Sunday mother baked a cake for me. It had three layers, and she tried to make it look like a cake from the Krakovsky confectionery. I knew she didn't have the patience to slice the cake horizontally because it crumbled. But this had lots of apricot jam between the layers with butter-cream and the top was sprinkled with chopped walnuts. She used real butter instead of margarine. She knew I could tell the difference and that I didn't like margarine in pastries.

At the end of dinner we all sat at the kitchen table enjoying dessert. My little sister, Gizi was looking forward to starting first grade in teacher Bozanich's class. Mother was happy I loved my cake and she let me eat as much as I wanted.

Father smiled at mother. "In July, Vili could spare his car for two weeks. He said, 'Bela, why don't you take your family on a vacation? I owe you so much.'"

Mother just looked at him, her eyes were shiny. It was rare that she remained speechless. She often scolded father for working on Vili's Fiat 750 for nothing. Once he got a few kilos of apples for a whole Saturday. Gizi climbed on father's lap clapping her hands, I hugged him and asked, "Are we going to watch the sunrise on the road?"

Mother laughed. "Of course. We have to find a room before they're all filled up."

That was a real trip if we left at dawn.

There were so many good gifts which made me happy. I loved them all.

Over Time:

It became a ritual to show my report card to father so he could see what I learned. We did that all the way through college. He always shook his head in disbelief and joy that I could store all that knowledge in my head. He said it was worth it for him to get up at dawn and work hard if his daughter was going to be this educated. He said in his time schools taught him to count, read, write, and history, not much more.

When I was in college he often asked me how this or that subject would help me to do my job. Neither of us knew the answer.

EPILOGUE

Why did I write these stories?

I have lived in the United States since the 1980's. My son was born in California and I often felt that his elementary and high school education was less broad than mine.

One day when he asked me, "Why do I need a college degree?" I realized I never asked this question when I had to choose a profession in Yugoslavia. Everyone attended college or some higher form of specialized education. It was the normal thing to do. I was to 'build a prosperous country because so many people died for our freedom.' I knew what I wanted, why I wanted it and what to do about it. I also knew I could do it no matter how difficult it would be.

I tried to remember what my parents and teachers told me so I could give some wisdom to my teenage son. Numerous events resurfaced from my childhood with the 'first time' experiences being the most vivid.

Sorting through my memories I was amazed how much power praise and criticism could have on a young child. I appreciated how my mother, father and teachers interpreted the world for me to see dignity, respect and gratitude. With adult eyes I understood my parents' love and fears and what motivated them.

I decided to put a handful of my stories in this book to share my experiences and perhaps inspire others to remember the moments of their vanished world. If childhood memories could bring a new understanding of who we are today, it's worth thinking about them. It was for me.

But I never found the wisdom I was looking for. How could I explain to my son the excitement and pride I felt, growing up with people that together built a better country, and that I, like so many others, would play an important role in the future? He never heard the songs and felt as I did, and he didn't understand that children, "little pioneers," could help win the war.

I told my son, "Get a college degree. You will figure out for yourself why you need it."

How was life in the Socialist Federal Republic of Yugoslavia (SFRY)?

Yugoslavia's social structure changed after WWII and people had to give up old traditions. An important part of the education was to teach children to speak in a 'modern way.' To convey specific phrases from my childhood I used literal translations instead of finding an English language equivalent.

I also kept the original spelling rules in salutations and addresses which were meant to reflect equality. For example, only names were capitalized when mentioned next to any profession because in our society the blacksmith was as valuable as the doctor. We wouldn't write Blacksmith Bezzegh or Doctor Bezzegh. She was teacher Bezzegh. The same was true for geographic names.

In the lower grades, from age seven through eleven we were like sponges, soaking up these rules we were taught. I wanted to be good, and that meant I followed what the adults told me. When I got in trouble for something it was because the rules in the school and at home were different. If my mother or teacher was angry or scared I didn't feel loved. I was sad and embarrassed for being 'bad' and learned that some rules were right for school and others were right for home.

At that age I didn't question the modern socialist values or old world traditions, I didn't think either one of them was better or worse. I only wanted to be a good kid, so I learned to live with two sets of values. The contradictions became clear by the time I turned into an opinionated teenager. But those are different stories for another time.

The role of arts and artists

One of the deepest marks the Pioneer Organization and the Communist Party left on us at that young age was that art wasn't valued. Even if you had talent, you might not get the chance to develop it. In my class several kids had talent for drawing, dancing, poetry, writing, but these skills were suitable only for hobbies and contests. They never encouraged us to pursue arts as life-long professions.

They tried to raise scientists, engineers, doctors, mechanics and qualified workers who would create a self-reliant socialist society. The purpose of 'the arts' was to spend quality time in theaters and museums, only as something to do after work.

Whether it was the philosophy at the time or a careful choice by the Party, they told us that you have to be born with talent to become an artist. You cannot learn art. We had very few schools for any type of art and the quota of new students would be around 12, while the allowable number of new students for electrical engineering or medicine would be 200 or more.

Decades later most of my classmates still nurtured their creativity and incorporated it in their lives as much as possible.

Heroes

As I grew up, my education included lots of stories about the partisans in WWII. One of the aims of the Pioneer Organization was to raise the new generations to respect the sacrifices of the partisans and anyone who fought for freedom. They taught us to be grateful and they succeeded, in a way. I remember feeling the awe and gratitude as a young child.

As time went by the constant repetitions turned this awe into 'just another partisan battle.' By the time we were in high school, we attended school dances where we couldn't wait to finish singing patriotic and folk songs just so we could put on a Beatles record or hum Terry Jacks' the 'Seasons in the Sun' and other rock-and-roll music.

Was communism a classless society?

Living in Yugoslavia during Josip Broz Tito's presidency meant different things to different people. For my working-class parents it was about building their home in a 'Garden City' and raising children who would have a college diploma and easier life. They told us to study and work hard. They had few or no opportunities for themselves, and had very limited money regardless how hard they worked.

Mother's plan to open a crepe kiosk at the farmer's market or any other request to start a small business was promptly denied or dismissed by the city government as an outrageous idea. Father never joined the Communist Party therefore he had no chance for promotions or privileges at work, yet he earned respect because of his work ethics. He was the last in line to get a raise, if any. His salary, like everyone else's, was constantly impacted by mandatory contributions for building bridges, viaducts, roads and railroads.

For most jobs, especially in education, it was mandatory to be in the Communist Party. My teachers had Party meetings, classroom inspections and directives about the curriculum such as the exact titles of the essays the students should write.

For my uncle who worked for the Yugoslav Air Force and got an apartment in Belgrade, his job meant following the strict rules of the Communist Party at all times. While my Godparents lived in a village, they attended Sunday church services, and their wealth depended on the land, the yield of the crops, and their private business.

In my experience, life in Yugoslavia greatly depended on individual ambitions and choices shaped by the war.

You could get a promotion but ...

Father was a teenager during WWII and had seen governments come and go. He saw money become worthless, and he experienced new rules, languages and cultures imposed by new regimes. He had to serve two-and-a-half-years in the newly formed Yugoslav Army. During that time Tito and Stalin broke up and Yugoslavia was expelled from the eastern bloc. In the army Father drove a tank and earned honors because he was skilled at fixing tanks and other vehicles. At the end of his term they offered him a job in the military. Father said, "No. Politics is not for me. I want to be my own man and live my life on my terms."

They asked him to reconsider because the job would put him on the fast track to becoming an officer. He would have to join the Communist Party. They offered him education, free housing, and high pay. He stood up and said, "No, thank you. I served my time for my country," then left. He was twenty-one years old. Throughout his life when similar promotions were offered to him, his answer remained the same, 'no politics.'

At the end it wasn't the Pioneer Organization or the Communist Party which played the most important role in my life. They set the direction and provided everything necessary to become an educated European citizen. I was proud of our multinational country. The six nations' and eight nationalities' diverse culture, music and cuisine created a sense of living in a very cosmopolitan Yugoslavia.

Ultimately my experiences were shaped by the love of my family, the dedication of the teachers, the laughter with my friends, connections with relatives, and the kindness of our neighbors. I learned that governments come and go but the relationships we build truly determine who we become.

Acknowledgements

I want to express my thanks and gratitude to:

My son, Jancsi for inspiration and his patience.
My family and friends, John, Sally, Jane and Mona whose questions and remarks helped me focus.
The Writers' Club of Whittier for its feedback and encouragement.
My editor, Sherry Barber for guiding me on how to keep cultural references while maintaining clarity.
The people in these stories, without whom I wouldn't be who I am today.

CPSIA information can be obtained
at www.ICGtesting.com
Printed in the USA
LVOW01s0230061216
515993LV00014B/544/P